The Beatles Guide to Love & Sex

How the Fab Four Inspired

a Cultural Revolution

Scott Robinson

The Beatles Guide to Love & Sex

Copyright © 2022 by Paleos Media
All rights reserved. Federal copyright law prohibits unauthorized reproduction by any means.

ISBN 979-8404034417

Cover art by Dan Smith
Cover design by Jim Wampler

Author photograph by Joshua Robinson

For Linda,

who first brought the lightning down on me in 1976 by playing "She's Leaving Home"...

Also by Scott Robinson ...

AI in Sci-Fi: Fictional Artificial Minds
    and the Real World Awaiting Them
The Children of Babel: Essays on the Inherent Nature of
    Artificial Intelligence and Consciousness
A Conversation with Hofstadter's Brain
Correct Me If I'm Wrong:
    Interdisciplinary (and Decidedly Speculative) Essays to
    Fill Idle Intellectual Moments
HAL 9000: An Unauthorized Biography
Red Brains, Blue Brains:
    Neuroscience and Donald Trump
Red Brains, Blue Brains: Authoritarian We Will Go!
A Chill in the Air: Profiles in American Authoritarianism
Lucy's Courtship: An Integrated Perspective
    on the Feminine Role in Human Sexual Evolution
Really Great Things That I Didn't Say
The Smell of the Lord (and Other Charming Heresies):
    Growing Up Fundamentalist in the American Midwest
Baby Boomer Fanboy: Growing Up in the Greatest Nerd Generation
The Heart of the Scots:
    Love, Sex and Romance in Scottish History
A Dark and Stormy Night in Scotland! Folk Tales, Legends, and
    Disturbing Bedtime Stories for the True Believer
Uncle Scott's Treasury of Useless Knowledge
Uncle Scott's Treasury of Random Information
Chasing the Enterprise:
    Achieving *Star Trek*'s Vision of the Human Future
Rock Candy: The Beatles
Rock Candy: Elton John
Rock Candy: Def Leppard
Rock Candy: Boston
The Quotable Beatles
To the Toppermost of the Poppermost:
    The #1 Hits of the Beatles, Before and After
The Progressive Beatles
The Classical Beatles
On the Yellow Brick Road:
    Analyzing the Music of Elton John, 1968-1977

More Than a Feeling:
>Analyzing the Music of Boston, 1976-1988

Yes Tales: An Unauthorized Biography
>of Rock's Most Cosmic Band

This Is What I'm Saying:
>Burdens of a Midwestern Suburban Polymath

My Work Here is Done!
>More Very Random Essays on Weighty Matters

I Think I'm Right in Saying That?
>The Intellectual Chaos Continues!

All My Thoughts, Unfiltered:
>Further Esoteric Explorations for Untethered Minds

I Think I've Said Quite Enough Already!
>Still More High-Quality Pablum for the Intellectually Ill-Nourished

For All Intensive Purposes

A Perpetual State of Randomness
>Further Adventures in Thematic Inconsistency!

Why Is He Telling Us This?
>The Best of Uncle Scott, 2012-2020

Ruminant: An Anthology of His Very Best

Don't Encourage Him!!! A Raucous Compendium of Irrelevance, Improprieties, and Serious Lapses In Judgment

Make Him Stop!!! A Second Raucous Compendium of Irrelevance, Improprieties, and Serious Lapses in Judgment

Shadows of Shadows

Table of Contents

Introduction   *1*

Prolog: 31 October 1956   *3*

Prolog: 15 July 1958   *5*

1957-1961: I Saw Her Standing There

Virgins in Liverpool   *8*

Cynthia Powell   *14*

Dot Rhone   *18*

Bad Boys in Hamburg   *21*

1962: With Love, From Me to You

Stu and Astrid   *28*

Scandal-Worthy   *32*

Wankers   *33*

Bye Bye, Heartthrob   *34*

The Pronoun Songs   *38*

"P.S. I Love You"   *42*

1963: I Want to Hold Your Hand

For the Love of Ringo   *46*

Jane Asher   *49*

"All My Loving"   *51*

John and Brian   *53*

1964: With a Love Like That, You Know You Should Be Glad

Satyricon   *60*

Pattie Boyd   *63*

"And I Love Her"   *65*

From Me to You: John and Cyn   *68*

"If I Fell"   *69*

1965: I Think I'm Gonna Be Sad

"Ticket to Ride"   *74*

"You've Got to Hide Your Love Away"   *76*

Papa Paul   *78*

"Help!"   *79*

"Yesterday"   *81*

The Women of *Rubber Soul*   *86*

"Norwegian Wood"   *88*

"If I Needed Someone"   *92*

"We Can Work It Out"   *94*

Love Letters on the Radio   *96*

"In My Life"   *103*

"Michelle / Girl"   *105*

"You Won't See Me"   *108*

"The Word"   *110*

1966: And When I Awoke, I Was Alone

"For No One"   *114*

"Here, There, and Everywhere"   *116*

Yoko Ono   *117*

"Love You To"   *120*

"She Said She Said"   *122*

1967: You're Gonna Lose That Girl

Beatlesogyny   *128*

"Lucy in the Sky with Diamonds"   *132*

From Me to You: Dear Jane   *136*

"When I'm Sixty-Four / Lovely Rita"   *140*

Beatlesex: Naughty Bits   *143*

"All You Need is Love"   *145*

Oedipus Rocks   *147*

"Lady Madonna"   *150*

Linda Eastman   *152*

1968: You Have Found Her, Now Go and Get Her

Breaking Up is Hard to Do: John and Cynthia   *158*

"Hey Jude"   *160*

Side Gigs   *163*

"Dear Prudence"   *170*

Breaking Up is Hard to Do: Paul and Jane   *172*

"Ob-La-Di, Ob-La-Da"   *174*

Apple Scruffs   *176*

"Happiness is a Warm Gun   *178*

For the Love of Pattie   *181*

"Don't Pass Me By"   *183*

You Say You Want a (Sexual) Revolution   *185*

"Julia"   *191*

1969: All I Have to Do is Think of Her

From Me to You: Pattie's Greatest Hits   *196*

"Don't Let Me Down"   *203*

"For You Blue"   *204*

Bros   *206*

"I Want You (She's So Heavy)"   *207*

"The Ballad of John and Yoko"   *210*

From Me to You: The Lovely Linda   *212*

"Something"   *214*

1970: Christ, You Know It Ain't Easy

From Me to You: John and Yoko   *218*

"The Long and Winding Road"   *220*

Swan Songs   *222*

And In the End...   *224*

Appendix: Beatlestats   *227*

Appendix: The Best Beatles Album to Have Sex To   *228*

Appendix: Beatle Babies   *232*

Appendix: *Love Songs*   *235*

Bibliography / Recommended Reading   *239*

The Beatles Guide to Love & Sex

Notes

Some of the quotations used are found in *The Quotable Beatles (4th Edition)*, by the author.

Several sub-chapters ("Dear Jane," "Beatle Babies," "Papa Paul," "Scandal-Worthy") are found in *Rock Candy: The Beatles*, also by the author.

Portions of the chapters "Norwegian Wood", "She Said She Said", "Yesterday", "Dear Prudence", "Happiness is a Warm Gun" and "I Want You (She's So Heavy)" were originally used in *The Progressive Beatles*, by the author.

Portions of the chapters "The Long and Winding Road" and "Something" were originally used in *To the Toppermost of the Poppermost*, by the author.

Introduction

During those brief years they were together, the Beatles had much to say about love.

The word *love*, in fact, occurs 613 times in the Beatles songbook. Eleven of their songs have *love* in the title. And of the 213 songs they gave us, more than half are love songs or relationship songs.

Every single single, in fact, from the first in 1962 ("Love Me Do") for almost four years was a love song, until "Paperback Writer" broke the streak in 1966.

We can surmise, then, that the Beatles knew an awfully lot about love.

Or did they?

Stepping back and looking at the Beatles as individuals, rather than songwriters, it's easy to wonder just how savvy they really were, when they first took the world by storm. Digging into their history, the subject of love grows increasingly murky, where the Fab Four are concerned.

We can, upon examination, defend the premise that when they started out, the greatest architects of the modern love song were really quite naïve and empty-headed – and that they took their sweet time growing into it. This progression can be generally charted as follows:

Indiscriminate horny teenagers ->
Vacuous celebrity pin-ups ->
Scandal-ridden cads ->
Devoted family men

As men and as artists, the Beatles present a rich and intriguing case study in the triumphs, uncertainties, vagaries, disappointments and outright failures of love, sex, and romance in the modern era. And it must be said, they did so without much intentionality; given their checkered personal histories, they were accidental lovers, at best.

From "I Saw Her Standing There", the Fabs presented as the coolest, most attentive, earnest, and eager lovers (to say nothing of the most desired) who ever broke into song; but the raw truth is that whatever success they found in this timeless domain emerged closer to the end of their run than the beginning.

John, for instance, was a mess from the start – jealous, insecure, and disingenuous;

Paul, it must be said, was by far the most eloquent and sure of himself, but also the least loving;

George echoed John's insecurities, but was easily more real and earnest than the other two;

And Ringo turns out to be the most forthright and honest lover of the bunch – but had no poetry whatsoever in his bosom.

A study of their music as it grew over their decade together, considered against the backdrop of their roller-coaster lives, gives us much to think about in the domain love.

So let's study and consider it!

STR
June 2022

"Prolog: 31 October 1956"

The Beatles Guide to Love & Sex

Mary McCartney had just turned 47. Receiving birthday wishes from family and friends, her smile hid a devastating reality, known to none of them, not even her sons Paul and Mike: she had just undergone a mastectomy – but the cancer had spread.

Only her husband Jim was privy to the horrible truth that the mastectomy had been for naught; the cancer had metastasized, traveling to her brain. She implored her husband to tell no one, not even their sons.

On October 29, Mary was admitted to David Lewis Northern Hospital, where her two boys, upon visiting, were still not told what was happening. It was the last time they would ever see their mother. Two days later, she was gone.

"I would have liked to have seen the boys growing up," were among her final words.

Jim went home and told his boys. Mike, at age 12 the younger of the two, burst into tears. Paul, 14, said, "How are we going to get by without her money?"

Insensitive as that sentiment sounds, its foundations were objectively valid. Mary was a nurse, and made more than Jim. The family income had just been reduced by more than half.

In retrospect, Paul himself was horrified at what he'd said.

"When I think back on it, I think, 'Oh God, *what*? Did I *really* say that?' It was a terrible, logical thought which was preceded by the normal feelings of grief. It was very tough to take."

It was a reaction that become standard for him. His response to John Lennon's assassination, 24 years later, would be a callous "It's a drag." Beatle biographer Mark Lewisohn interpreted:

"Paul's way of dealing with the crisis was to seem unaffected by it," he wrote. "He just carried on. 'I learned to put a shell around me.' Tough as it was to see or hear his dad crying, Paul got his head down and pushed forward."

Paul had inherited that get-on-with-it detachment, at least in part, from Mary herself: she was warm and calm at home, around Paul and Mike – but, as a nurse, would frequently be called out on the spur of the moment to deliver a baby. She would immediately shift into work mode, packing her nursing gear and heading out to get it done. That immediate shifting of gears, tucking one's emotions in a carry bag, took root in Paul.

Even so, those close to him knew he'd been deeply wounded by her sudden death. "Paul was far more affected by Mum's death than any of us imagined," his brother Mike later said. "His very character seemed to change and for a while he seemed like a hermit. He wasn't very nice to live with at this period, I remember. He became completely wrapped up in himself and didn't want people breaking in on his life."

However he had processed his feelings about her death, Paul's memories of his mother offer a portrait of a vibrant, loving woman:

"She was very kind, very loving," he remembered. "There was a lot of sitting on laps and cuddling. I think I was very close to her. She liked to joke and had a good sense of humor and she was very warm. There was more warmth in her than I now realise there was in most families."

Paul McCartney became a different person. The loss of the woman who had shown him, through the example of her life and love, the kind of man he could grow up to be, became a permanent scar inside him. He would never be able to deal with death; and in his own relationships, a part of him would always be guarded.

Mary's death shaped not only her future son, but the world-renowned songwriter and generational emissary he was destined to become.

"Prolog: 15 July 1958"

John Lennon's friend Nigel Walley went round to the home of John's Aunt Mimi on Menlove Avenue, with whom John lived – and found, instead, John's mother Julia, having tea with her sister. Ironically, John wasn't there, but was at his mother's house. She was ready to head back home, and so she and Nigel walked toward the bus stop near Mimi's. She was in a fun mood, cracking jokes with the boy as evening fell. They parted ways before the bus stop, as he had decided to head home.

Julia impulsively jaywalked, crossing Menlove Avenue between corners. Several dozen yards away, Nigel heard a screech of tires and a horrifying thud, and turned to see Julia's body flying through the air.

An off-duty policeman in a car hadn't seen her, and had hit her head-on. Her body traveled almost 100 feet from where she'd been hit.

"I ran back to get Mimi," Nigel reported, "and we rushed to wait for the ambulance."

Just after 11 p.m., a policeman knocked on Julia's door and gave young John – then 17 – the news. He and Julia's partner Bobby Dykins took a taxi to Sefton General Hospital. Refusing to see his mother's body, Dykins was sent in to identify her.

Julia had turned John over to Mimi to raise in his early boyhood – and his father Freddie, described by Beatle biographer Bob Spitz as "a screwup," had never been around. John was now truly on his own.

Though Julia had not been a full-time mother to John, he didn't lack for love, growing up; his Aunt Mimi and Uncle George were very much there for him, and Julia – who remained close to her sister – visited frequently. Ironically, at the time of her death, she and John had grown closer than ever, according to Spitz:

"Though tainted by the past, John and Julia had gravitated naturally toward each other and at this point in their lives welcomed the closeness that, by all accounts, they'd missed out on earlier. Now in her mid-forties, Julia finally had the wherewithal – the ability and enthusiasm, as well as the influence – to counsel her son, and she provided the perfect ear for John's mounting anxieties."

"It was the worst thing that ever happened to me," John remembered. "We'd caught up so much, me and Julia, in just a few years. We could communicate. We got on. She was great. I thought, 'Fuck it, fuck it, fuck it. That's really fucked everything. I've no responsibilities to anyone now."

John's lifelong friend Pete Shotton said that John's relationship with his mother as he grew was "a source of unending confusion, much as he tried to give the impression of taking it all in his stride."

Biographer Albert Goldman suggests that Julia's death stirred more than grief in her son: "The effects of Julia's death were grave," he wrote. "Beneath his grief burned a terrible rage ignited by the recognition that once again he had been abandoned by his mother."

John didn't speak to Nigel for months, somehow blaming the whole thing on him.

Julia Lennon died just over a year after John had befriended Paul McCartney – who had, in turn, lost his own mother a little less than a year before that. The mutual loss became a bond between them.

"Now we were both in this," Paul said, "both losing our mothers. This was a bond for us, something of ours, a special thing. We'd both gone through that trauma and both come out the other side... we could look at each other and know."

The legacy of Julia's sudden death, at the time John needed her most, would be a fear and dread that would define him for decades – and shape the artist he would become, in blatant and vulnerable ways that would find resonance in millions of those who would one day embrace his music.

1956-1961:

I Saw Her Standing There

Virgins in Liverpool

Any account of the Beatles as men of their times, cultural trendsetters - or even simply as husbands and boyfriends - must, necessarily, begin at the beginning: they were once horny young teenagers.

There's a wondrous, confusing, often traumatic archive in the mind of every adult male, be he a legendary lover, dutiful family man, or luckless lounge lizard – a place that predates memories of the scent of a woman, successful intimate encounters, horrific romantic errors and painful break-ups. It's an archive of bloated and outlandish expectations, ignorance-driven misperceptions, outsized fantasies and just plain bad information – a corner of the male mind that will rapidly be overshadowed by brutal reality, but which will persist, embarrassingly, throughout his days.

What does this precarious stretch of tortured innocence matter? Why is this period of rude and awkward awakening important?

Most men, whatever their relative rate of success in life as they have pursued the art of love, will attest that those early successes and failures that populate this corner of memory, the ridiculous (and sometimes precarious) attempts at connection, self-reinvention, and oh-so-tentative exploration often have a tremendous impact on the man they often become.

And so it was in the minds of four wide-eyed innocents in the seaside city of Liverpool in the mid-to-late Fifties. In their earliest interactions with the opposite sex, we can see traces of the men they will eventually become – men who will, for better or worse, end up with a great deal to say (to a *very* big audience) about women and love and sex and their role in all of it.

We can begin with John, who presents as bolder that the others in their formative years. Even in his mid-teens, he had begun deploying the hot-cold swings in behavior and attitude toward women that would continue throughout his too-brief life. Those swings, well-documented, had the adult John vacillating between romantic sweetheart and abusive tormenter. The young John wasn't much different.

These swings first occurred with girlfriend Barbara Baker, whom John got serious about in high school – or as serious as he was able to be. He had known Barbara since they were small children together in Sunday School, and had not exactly endeared himself; she would later recall that he shot arrows at her, perched in a tree, as she walked home from school, and that he and his best pal Pete Shotton laughingly called her "horse face."

The last laugh was hers, as she grew into a stunning teenage beauty, and the fundamentally insecure John radically changed his tune. Making a point to dress smartly, he began chatting her up (a practice he'd mastered already, in pursuit of his first coital triumph[1]) after class, and soon they began bike riding and ice skating together.

"He was a very romantic boy, extremely romantic," she would later recall.[2] "He wrote pages and pages of poetry to me. 'Here,' he would say, 'I've written you a letter, a poem – read it!'"

This would culminate in her annexation of his virginity. She had experience that he didn't, leading him to later identify her as "an older woman," even though they were the same age.

"Well, Pete," he told Shotton,[3] "I've had me first screw. I had a hell of a job getting inside Barb. It was like trying to get inside a mouse's earhole. Actually, I think, I'd rather have a wank."

Poetry, indeed.

John and Barb remained a couple, more or less, for the next two years, through the formation of the pre-Beatles group The Quarrymen and the beginning of John's friendship with Paul. Eventually Barb ended it.

---

[1] He recorded his attempts in a diary his Aunt Mimi discovered. Had it survived, it surely would be a *New York Times* bestseller.

[2] Chronicled in Marc Shapiro's *Beatle Wives*.

[3] In Shotton's *John Lennon In My Life*.

"I cooled off on him," she remembered, "and started going out with [his friend Bill Turner] behind his back. John went crazy. He nearly kicked a fence in that night."

John later took up with a young woman named Thelma Pickles, early in his college days. Described as "shy and sensitive," Thelma was nonetheless very straightforward – and even bold at times. Overhearing another girl casually referencing John's mother's death, she sought him out and commiserated with him over their mutual abandonment by their fathers. Their shared loss became the basis of a relationship.

"What I realized quickly," she would remember, "was that he and I had an aggression towards life that stemmed entirely from our home lives. We couldn't wait to grow up and tell everyone to get lost."[4]

"He certainly didn't have a romantic attitude to sex," Thelma reported later. "He had a very disparaging attitude to girls who wanted to be involved with him but wouldn't have sex with him.[5] He was no different than any young bloke. If he felt you were leading him on but would not have sex with him, he'd be very abusive. With John it was entirely about lust."[6]

Moreover, Thelma managed to resist John's attempts to inseminate her for precisely that reason – and the fact that she wisely feared getting pregnant.

And in his frustration, the now-17-year-old John turned to another fellow student – Cynthia Powell.

Though the young Paul displayed the possessiveness that would define his relationships throughout his life, he was, by the accounts of his early girlfriends, more gentlemanly than his bandmate. The first of these was a girl named Layla, with whom he took up briefly at age 15 (she was older, and in his recollection, very well-endowed). She would invite him to baby-

[4] In Goldman, *The Lives of John Lennon*.

[5] Per Goldman, John called such girls "spaniels".

[6] In Shapiro, *Beatle Wives*.

sit with her, which meant having a house to themselves for a few hours – an opportunity to fool around. This generally didn't go well, as the danger of being caught was not trivial, and would have resulted in disgrace.

Others would follow, including a girl named Julie Arthur, niece of the popular BBC comedian Ted Ray. Paul, already a charmer, fielded considerable feminine interest as a Quarryman, and lamented that teenage love in Liverpool was as challenging as it was in the US Midwest – the problem was, where to go to fool around? His easy smile and good humor got them interested, but he had nowhere to take them.

And there were other challenges. One young woman he found himself alone with was, upon examination, wearing a girdle, which he found perplexing: "Fumbling teenage fingers, it was a damn good barrier."[7]

And then, at the Casbah Club, where The Quarrymen made their name, a young woman named Dot Rhone approached both John and Paul one evening and introduced herself – and soon became Paul's first long-term girlfriend.

Teenage John was bold and selfish; teenage Paul was charming and opportunistic. It was George who turned out to be the true gentleman. And a chaste one, at that: while his older bandmates managed to lose their virginity in their hometown (however awkwardly), George wouldn't get past third base until The Quarrymen toured Germany.

Prior to that, his interest in girls had blossomed around age 14, when he'd briefly gone steady with a 12-year-old friend named Jennifer Brewer – watching television and holding hands.[8] Even then, his interest in girls was secondary to his interest in the guitar: "He was now mad about music," Brewer recalled. "He loved things like Elvis with a passion."

---

[7] In Barry Miles' *Many Years from Now*.

[8] In Shapiro's *Beatle Wives*.

So it was with the next girlfriend, Ruth Morrison, with whom he managed to advance to kissing. But she, too, fell by the wayside as his dedication to music intensified.

Then came a young woman with whom he could combine his interests: Iris Caldwell, the little sister of Alan Ernest Caldwell – who, as Rory Storm, was frontman of the regionally famous band Rory Storm and the Hurricanes.

"He was really into me or so I thought," Iris said. "But, in hindsight, I think the main reason was he was trying to get into my brother's band."

If so, it didn't work: Rory rejected George as a potential band member. But that point was moot: very soon, Paul and John recruited him for The Quarrymen.

George and Iris continued hanging out together beyond Rory's rejection, and there came an evening when Rory's band was playing at a club and he said something horrible to his sister, sending her running out of the club in tears. George was with her, and his gentlemanly side emerged.

"I just ran out of the place in hysterics," she recalled, "and I could hear these footsteps behind me and all of a sudden they caught up with me and the person turned me around and it was George. That was our first kiss and it was the best kiss of my life. To this day I still remember that feeling in my tummy. Nobody ever kissed me like that. It was beautiful."[9]

Ringo, at the time, wasn't yet Ringo[10] – he was still just Richy Starkey. And he had yet to meet any of his future Beatle brothers.

His own romantic adventures had included an aspiring hairstylist named Patricia Davis, who had met Ringo's mum Elsie

---

[9]Ibid.

[10]Ringo became Ringo in late 1959, upon getting the gig George had longed for – a place among Rory Storm's Hurricanes. Richy Starkey, already known as "Rings" because he always wore at least four, took the easy next step to "Ringo" as a stage name – shortening his last name to "Starr" at the same time, much to Rory's delight.

in her quest to find women who would trust her to do their hair. "She let us bleach her hair and do terrible things to it," she remembered, "but she never once complained... Mrs. Starkey was a fantastic lady!" She also recalled the high level of hospitality of the Starkey home.[11]

His first truly serious relationship was with Geraldine McGovern, an attractive furniture factory worker whom he met at Litherton Town Hall (a future Beatles venue) in 1957. He became a regular presence in the McGovern family's Kent Gardens, to her parents' approval. Her father described them as "inseparable."[12]

Even so, Ringo shared George's priorities: music came first. Even though his relationship to Gerry stretched three years, proceeding to engagement and a wedding date, "His music always came first. He was playing most nights and if I wanted to see him, I had to go along with him. We were never able to have much time together."

Things came to a head between them when Gerry began pressuring Ringo to leave Rory Storm and the Hurricanes and get a proper job, so they could proceed to marriage. The band was booked to do a residency at a summer camp, meaning a long separation.

"That really ruined the relationship when he went off to that job," she said. "I told him I didn't want him to go. We talked it over. There was no shouting or slagging. But that was the end."

"I did love her and she loved me," Ringo said much later.[13]

We begin, then, with four portraits of artists as young men, all eager to partner up, but even more eager to pursue the muse. And we can see, even in these teenage years, what kind of boyfriends and husbands they were destined to become.

---

[11]In Michael Seth Starr's *Ringo: With a Little Help*.

[12]Ibid.

[13]In Shapiro's *Beatle Wives*.

Cynthia Powell

In the Beatles long-term relationship department, Cynthia Powell would be considered the elder statesperson.

She was the first, of course. She was, in the band's early years, by far the most consequential. And she would become, over time, the most tragic.

John had had several casual girlfriends by the time he met Cynthia in a calligraphy class at the Liverpool College of Art in September 1957. Cynthia was unlike any of them; refined and reserved, she was a new experience altogether.

He, on the other hand, "was a real scruff, a real Teddy Boy," she told the *Sun*, "who always dressed in black and always had a guitar with him. He looked as if he would punch you just as soon as look at you. As soon as he walked into class, you could tell he didn't want to be there."

Cynthia had lost her father to lung cancer the previous year, which gave the abandoned John something in common with her. He called her "Miss Prim," and the two began spending time together. Both were instinctively wary; but after months of casual association, John finally asked her out.

Cynthia deflected, claiming to be engaged. This pissed John off: "I didn't ask you to fucking marry me, did I?" After he cooled off, he circled back, asking her to join him at a pub with friends. She regretted the deflection, so she went along. That very night, they kissed, went to the flat of a friend of John's, and had sex.

And, just like that, they were a couple.

"When you're very young, love is very blind," she wrote later. "I had no idea what was going to happen. We were living for the moment and that's the way it should have been and it was. So I didn't know."

One advantage they had, as they entered into couplehood, was having spent months as friends, talking about their lives. Cynthia already knew all about John's past, his father's absenteeism and his mother's death. She knew what she was getting into, and was able to be a good partner early on, despite having little experience with young men like him.

"He was very raw inside and full of pain, emotional pain," she told author Chris Hunt. "I think he really relied on me, and he kept testing me to make sure I was constant and that I wouldn't do anything to hurt him or harm him." This insecurity would soon surface in his songwriting.

John's Aunt Mimi was not a fan. She referred to Cynthia as "a gangster's moll," and once threw a hand mirror at John when she learned he'd spent a great deal of money on a suede coat for Cynthia.

John wasn't exactly the most experienced partner, and immediately ran into difficulty processing his emotions. He was jealous and possessive, and this brought out a violence in him that hadn't surfaced before. Walking into a room at school and finding her dancing with his friend Stu Sutcliffe, he immediately jumped to the wrong conclusion.

"Out of nowhere he just smacked me across the face and I hit my head against a pipe," she reported to the *Sun*. That was it, as far as she was concerned. She ended the relationship on the spot.

Three months later, he called her and begged for another chance.

"He was desperately sorry," she recalled. "It was just an instant and he couldn't help himself. He didn't do it again and I wouldn't have been with him if he had. It was the first and last time he lifted a finger to me."

He would, as events unfolded, find other ways to hurt her.

Arriving in John's life when she did, Cynthia had a courtside seat from which to watch the emergence of the Beatles, from their early Quarrymen days into superstardom. She was there in the early club days; she was there during the early Germany tours; for the line-up changes that preceded the Fab Four; for the record label auditions.

And it was just as the band was connecting with producer George Martin and beginning a real career, in the summer of 1962, that she got pregnant.

"Cynthia had often acknowledged to a highly active and spontaneous sex life, often conducted in alleys and doorways, and that birth control had never been a thought," wrote biographer Marc Shapiro.

"There was no planning," biographer Ray Coleman quoted her in *Lennon*. "There was no pill in those days. We considered nothing except ourselves and didn't consider the consequences. We weren't thinking about anything like prevention."

She remembered telling John: "Feeling very sick and faint, with all the fight knocked out of me, I broke the news to John," she wrote in *A Twist of Lennon*. "After tearfully blurting out the results of my examination by the doctor, I watched his face drain of all its colour, and fear and panic creep into his eyes. He was speechless for what seemed like an age. I stared at him, my heart pounding so fast I thought I would pass out. Finally John broke the interminable silence:

"There's only one thing for it, Cyn," he said. "We'll have to get married."

The first Beatle wedding was modest and relatively secretive, becoming the model for those to follow. Manager Brian Epstein, obsessed with keeping a lid on the event, made all the arrangements and kept things very private.

"Accounts of our wedding have often portrayed it as a miserable last-minute shotgun affair that John was virtually forced into," Cynthia wrote in *John*. Again, it's a long, long way from the truth. It was last-minute, which meant that we had no flowers, no reception, no beautiful dress and no photographer, but it wasn't miserable. In fact, it was the opposite: we were very happy."

Epstein was dapper when he picked Cynthia up in a chauffeur-driven car on the rainy day they married, in a nondescript civil ceremony. John was downright giddy, despite the weather. George kept the mood lighter still, stepping forward when the registrar called for the groom to do so. Paul served as one of the official witnesses.

John tried earnestly to be a good newlywed husband, bringing her flowers and encouraging her through her pregnancy. Cynthia recalled one day when he came home from a gig and had her close her eyes while he brought in a gift. It was an old coffee table he'd managed to acquire for only five pounds. "Despite my misgivings about it, I couldn't help but be swept along by his enthusiasm," she wrote.

On tour with the band, John missed the birth of his son Julian, finally arriving at the hospital three days later.

"He came in like a whirlwind, racing through the doors in his haste to find us," Cynthia wrote. "He kissed me, then looked at his son, who was in my arms. There were tears in his eyes: 'Cyn, he's bloody marvelous! He's fantastic.' He sat on the bed and I put the baby into his arms. He held each tiny hand, marveling at the miniature fingers, and a big smile spread over his face. 'Who's going to be a famous little rocker like his dad, then?' he said."

And so it went. Before the band truly broke, and seemingly no time at all since John had been a teenage Teddy Boy in Liverpool, there was now a husband and father among the Beatles.

This became a pattern. And part of the pattern was that in Beatleworld, wives and children would be secret, so as not to enrage the band's female fan base; thus spake Brian Epstein.

"I was still a secret, and I hated it," Cynthia wrote in *John*. "I wanted to be acknowledged as John's wife. Of course, some of the Liverpool fans knew, but to the rest of the country he was young, free, and single. Every now and then when I was out with Julian in the pram a girl would come up and ask whether I was John's wife. I had to play up to the role I'd been assigned, say no, and hurry off."

Dot Rhone

Dorothy "Dot" Rhone had made the first move with Paul, walking right up to him and John at the Casbah Club one night between Quarrymen sets in 1959. This forward behavior was somewhat typical of the women in the Beatles' lives, even early on – and decidedly *a*-typical for the era.[14]

Dot was 16 at the time she made this bold move, which had actually been directed at John, rather than Paul; but she quickly learned that John was spoken for, and set her sights on his songwriting partner.

"Paul was handsome in a softer way than John. I liked that," she later said. "So we were sitting around talking and I said I felt a bit woozy, that I might faint, and went outside. Paul came out after me to see if I was all right, and it was then that he said, 'D'you fancy going out?' That had been my plan and it worked."

Dot herself was "a sweet-faced blonde," per Mark Lewisohn, "quiet and innocent." John nicknamed her Bubbles, "because she wasn't."

But she knew what she wanted. And she decided she wanted Paul.

Paul had never been serious about anyone before Dot. It was this relationship that set the tone for the partner he would become – romantic and kind on the one hand, possessive and controlling on the other.

On the kind side, Paul would write letters to her when he and the band went on the first Hamburg tour in 1960. He bought her a gold ring there and brought it home to her. On the controlling side, he picked out her clothes for her and insisted she adopt the hair style of Bridgitte Bardot, after whom he and John were constantly lusting. He discouraged her from seeing her friends, and pushed her to stop smoking, even though he himself continued.

"He was so possessive that he needed to control everything about me," she would later report, "my appearance, the way I

---

[14]Maureen Cox, who would end up marrying Ringo, used exactly this strategy two years later.

dressed, even the way I thought. He was always wanting me to look better than I did, and I never thought I measured up to the way I thought I should be. Back then I went along with it. I became his puppet."

"She was very much in love with Paul," said her friend Sandra Hedges. "He in turn would jealously guard her by placing her amid the group while they were playing."

Even so, "Dot Rhone loved being Paul McCartney's girlfriend," Lewisohn wrote. "He was unusual and a cut above the other boys: much better-looking, brighter, sharper, musically gifted, an entertaining mimic. It did entail acquiescing to a few demands... he didn't want her to see any of her friends, he didn't want her to smoke (though he did), and he copied John by insisting on her adoption of the Brigitte Bardot look."

"He gave me a list of rules that I had to stick to," Dot recalled. "John had the same rules for Cynthia."

Then, in February 1960, Dot discovered she was pregnant.

She was 16. He was 17. At that young age, it wasn't uncommon to give babies conceived under such circumstances up for adoption, but Paul instead proposed marriage. They would live with his father, who loved the idea of being a grandfather.

But about three months into the pregnancy, Dot miscarried. She remembered being at the hospital, where Paul came to see her.

"He seemed a bit upset," she remembered, "but deep down he was probably relieved."

The two remained a couple, but talk of marriage ended.

She and Cynthia became close, a sort of big sister-little sister relationship. At the time of the pregnancy, Dot had moved into the house where Cynthia was living. They kept each other company when the boys were off playing in Germany, though – oddly – Dot didn't divulge her pregnancy to Cynthia at the time.

And so it went, until the time came when John and Paul opened up to the idea of Cynthia and Dot joining them on a Hamburg trip. That happened in 1962.

Paul and Dot stayed in a bungalow by the Hamburg docks, and in his off time took Dot sightseeing. He bought her gifts, including a gold ring, and treated her like a queen. He was honest about having other girls in Hamburg, but insisted that he wasn't serious about any of them; they were strippers, one and all, and he and the other Beatles indulged in them only because they knew more about sex than girls back home. If you were going to be the girlfriend of a Beatle, you had to be okay with that.

Her relationship with Paul continued into the fall, until - in the wake of John and Cynthia's marriage - she made clear that she too wanted to be married. He made clear that he didn't.

And that was that.

Bad Boys in Hamburg

"It was as if they'd gone off to war," Dot said, referring to the separations she and Cynthia endured when the band went on tour in Hamburg. John and Paul would dutifully write them long, florid letters expressing their undying love and impatience to be reunited (this would become a central theme in Paul's songwriting). Beyond the view of their girlfriends back home, however, they were having the time of their lives.

"Presumably, Dot and Cynthia knew the score," wrote biographer Bob Spitz. "Hamburg's earthly delights were legendary, especially now that so many musicians had returned home. Neither had any illusions about the Beatles' fidelity. As Cynthia expressed it, 'John was a flirt.' But it seems doubtful she understood the full extent of his exploits. 'As long as they were happy, we were happy,' Dot says."

Spitz wrote that in Hamburg, "girls came out of the woodwork... There was a girl for everybody, and not just edge-of-the-bed virgins, like back home. These girls were polished, stylish, smart, and fashionable. The musicians were invited to the homes of their German girlfriends, introduced to approving mothers, and then hauled upstairs to bed."

The Beatles' first exposure to this "first-class orgy" began in August 1960, when promoter Allan Williams had been blown off by both Rory Storm and Gerry and the Pacemakers and needed to send someone over fast. The Beatles were a last-minute fill-in, in his mind.

"The Beatles were home in Hamburg," said Adrian Barber of the Casanovas. "It was their town." There would be four Hamburg expeditions altogether: that first one in 1960, another the following spring, another one year after that, and a final one in late 1962.

"My first shag was in Hamburg with John, Paul and Pete watching," he recalled in *Behind Sad Eyes: The Life of George Harrison*. "We were in bunk beds and they really couldn't see anything because I was under the covers. But after I finished, they applauded and cheered. At least they kept quiet whilst I was doing it."

That account squares with Paul's memory, shared with *GQ* in 2018:

"I think that's true... The thing is, these stories, particularly Beatles stories, they get to be legendary, and I do have to check: Wait a minute. I know we had one bed and two sets of bunks, and if one of the guys brought a girl back, they could just be in the bed with a blanket over them, and you wouldn't really notice much except a little bit of movement. I don't know whether that was George losing his virginity—it might have been. I mean, I think in the end this was one of the strengths of the Beatles, this enforced closeness which I always liken to army buddies. Because you're all in the same barracks. We were always very close and on top of each other, which meant you could totally read each other."

The first trip ended badly, with Paul and Pete accused of arson and deported, while George was sent home for being under-age (he was only 17). But in the spring of 1961, they headed back.

"Sex was everywhere, and figured high on the Beatles' menu," wrote Mark Lewisohn. "There was no change they'd match the fidelity demanded of girlfriends back home. And yet, because so much happened to the Beatles in Hamburg – and because, supposedly, every excess was available here so easily – detaching fact from fiction just isn't possible. As John would reflect in 1980, 'There was a lot of heavy *boys' fun* when we were in Hamburg, but the stories built out of all proportion – over the years they became like *legends*'... and, after 1980, those legends would grow exponentially.

"To give just one example, Pete Best – an honest man, prone to understatement rather than exaggeration – has talked of all the Beatles having sex simultaneously at the Bambi Kino, but George, speaking of the unforgettable occasion he lost his virginity, clearly describes John, Paul and Pete being in the room at the same time, in bunk beds, which was a 1961 situation. Accordingly, as unlikely as this is, it appears George managed to go through the entire, extraordinary experience of 1960 without having sex, despite the mass of opportunities, a healthy sexual appetite and Stu describing him in print as a Casanova."

"The Beatles were a bunch of randy sods and they suddenly found themselves in a sexual paradise," wrote McCartney biographer Chet Flippo. "It's not surprising that they would attract female followers. They were young, good-looking, playing sexy music in the open sex capital of Europe, and they made no secret of the fact that they were open to sex. Paul and John, especially, and mostly Paul because of his cherubic looks, were objects of terrific sexual desire. Even the transvestites from the queer bars came around for a try on these hot Liverpool lads. Good-looking teenagers in tight clothes singing hot rock 'n' roll and throwing their young bodies all across the stage? Forget it. The demand was there. As Pete Best later said, they didn't realize until they got to Hamburg that there were an infinite number of young women out there who would literally do anything for them. Anything. Just because they were Beatles. And this was before they were really famous."

Lewisohn notes that Hamburg provided "plenty of action – mostly with barmaids and sometimes with strippers." And he further noted that "the Beatles became very close, tighter than ever, here in Hamburg. There was no privacy and they all witnessed the others in intimate situations. As Paul says, 'I'd walk in on John and see a little bottom bobbing up and down with a girl underneath him. It was perfectly normal: you'd go, "Oh shit, sorry," and back out of the room.'"

Paul further recalled, in a 2018 *GQ* interview, "I remember there was someone in a club that he'd met, and they'd gone back to the house because the wife fancied John, wanted to have sex with him, so that happened... John discovered the husband was watching. That was called 'kinky' in those days."

Pete Best was the exception. He "conducted his private life privately, as was his way," according to Lewisohn. "He went to where the women lived, and was spending much offstage time with a stripper whose husband was in jail."

Further, per Lewisohn, Pete was more sensible than his bandmates – just one of the many ways he didn't fit in well. He was concerned, for instance, that the loose sex of Hamburg might easily saddle one with a bad case of venereal disease, writing to a friend, "Over here you have got to be so damn careful if you go for your oats. The only snag is, the way they throw it at you, it's just impossible to resist – especially after you have got a few bevvies inside of you. Anyway I'm trying my best at the moment not to bring home any 'you know whats' - come to think of it, it's worth the risk because I'm dreading coming home to those 'things' that call themselves girls in the clubs."

Then there was the time when John was on top of a girl in the Beatles' quarters as a man named Horst Fascher, a kind of sex cop enforcing an old German decency law called *Kuppeleiparagraph*, came upon them and tried to separate them. He was unable to do so, and opted to force the issue by urinating on them. John surged to his feet, livid, but hesitated to engage Fascher, who had once done time for manslaughter.

And there was John's dalliance with barmaid Bettina Derlien, whose breasts were so large that putting one's head between them "was a nice way to go deaf for a few seconds," according to Pete, who actually tried it.

This raucous history emphasizes the curiosity and audacity that the boys from Liverpool harbored from their earliest days. They were anxious to see the world and try new things, and this would later serve them well as both artists and cultural heralds.

It also, however, normalized some of their worst impulses; Hamburg was a kind of amplifier stack which, once they plugged into it, greatly intensified their self-indulgence and willingness to wall themselves off from any intimacy that approached. Their four excursions were surely great adventures, and filled with dangerous fun; but their behavior in that world had opened doors that would make their lives more complicated – particularly when they began touring the entire world.

"We had a bond there that we never talked about – but each of us knew that had happened to the other... I know he was shattered, but at that age you're not *allowed* to be devastated and particularly as young boys, teenage boys, you just shrug it off. That's a lot of what we did – we had private tears. It's not that either of us were remotely hard-hearted about it, it *shattered* us, but we knew you had to get on with your life. I'm sure I formed shells and barriers in that period that I've got to this day. John certainly did."

~Paul, speaking of the deaths of his mother Mary and John's mother Julia

The Beatles Guide to Love & Sex

1962:

With Love, From Me to You

Stu and Astrid

As the romantic errors and over-the-top indulgences of the Fab Four pile up in the ensuing pages, it's important to remember this: in their early days, when the band was new and their personal traumas were tragically fresh and they were bouncing around Europe immersing themselves in self-destructive behaviors, they nonetheless had access to an exemplary template of love and relationship done well – the proverbial Real Thing - right under their noses.

That template consisted of original Beatles bassist Stu Sutcliffe and his German fiancée, photographer Astrid Kirchherr.

Astrid, at 22, had been a student at Meisterschulefür Mode in Hamburg, with hopes of studying fashion design. She was already a brilliant photographer, specializing in black-and-white photography, and was given a job as assistant to the school's top photography tutor.

She and several of her fellow art students – Jürgen Vollmer and Klaus Voorman in particular – joined the European existentialist movement and took to dressing in black, looking moody, and hanging around in France. Call them Early Emo.

Astrid and Klaus were a couple at the time he happened to wander into Hamburg's Kaiserkeller Club and see five British rockers on stage. This was 1960, so the early incarnation of the Beatles he'd stumbled upon included John, Paul, George, Pete Best on drums - and Stu Sutcliffe on bass.

He returned to the club with Astrid and Jürgen in tow, and Astrid decided immediately that this was a crowd she wanted to hang with.

Seeing the Beatles for the first time, "It was like a merry-go-round in my head, they looked absolutely astonishing," she remembered. "My whole life changed in a couple of minutes. All I wanted was to be with them and to know them."

Astrid was, to say the least, beautiful – petite with short blonde hair, and eyes to get lost in. If the Beatles had grabbed her attention, she grabbed theirs in turn. Particularly Stu's.

This early version of the Beatles had arisen from the Quarrymen, with Stu (who couldn't yet play an instrument) convinced by John and Paul to buy a bass and join the band not long before their name- change to the Beatles. Stu had come to know John from the art school they'd both attended, and were good friends – closer than John and Paul were, even then.

Their three new German friends rapidly identified Stu as the odd man out in the Beatles; they knew an artist when they saw one. And, of course, Stu already realized he didn't fit in with the John/Paul aesthetic.

"They could see immediately, they said," Stu shared in a letter to a friend. "Here was I, feeling the most insipid working member of the group being told how much superior I looked – this along side the great Romeo John Lennon and his two stalwarts Paul and George – the casanovas of Hamburg!"

Stu never got very good on the bass, and was encouraged by other art school voices to drop music and focus on art. He hadn't listened to them.

But he was all ears, where Astrid was concerned. He worked up the courage to ask her out after she convinced the band to do a photo shoot with her, and they became a couple thereafter. Klaus Voormann politely stepped aside, without jealousy, becoming friends with the band himself.

Stu's new relationship "peeved the rest of us like mad," Paul later said, "that she hadn't fallen in love with any of us. It was something none of us had ever seen before. None of our parents had that sort of relationship."

This is an important point. The love that flourished so suddenly and wondrously between quiet Stu and their new German friend Astrid took the other Beatles very much by surprise; and its quality and overt depth was a far cry from their teddy-boy romances back home, and farther still from the cheap and shallow liaisons they indulged in abroad.

It inserted a thread of uncertainty, and perhaps even fraud, into the soaring, enchanting love song lyrics John and Paul were grinding out. Here they were, composing odes to romance and deep, undying love between a young man and woman (having never experienced it themselves) – and it was being lived out, earnestly and gloriously, right in front of them.

Pete Best would go on to describe Stu and Astrid's relationship as "one of those fairy stories," in the classic romantic tradition. They became engaged in November 1960, and Astrid would call Stu "the love of my life."

Just before their engagement, Stu had actually written a letter to his parents, asking their permission to propose to Astrid. In that letter, he wrote:

"I've loved before but never so tenderly and intensely. The last three weeks or so have been a dream."

When their late-1960 Hamburg tour was upset by Paul, Pete and George's deportation, John and Stu were trapped in Hamburg. John made it home to England, but Stu stayed behind with Astrid. Not long after, he returned home to Liverpool, taking Astrid with him to meet his family.

Not long after, Stu and Astrid had their first period apart, with her back home in Hamburg while he played in England with the Beatles. In one of the many letters he wrote her during those few weeks, he confessed to wearing her jeans and blue pullover on stage (they were about the same size) – and drew a cartoon of himself as a visual aid.

That summer, Stu acquiesced to the voices urging him to devote himself to art. He quit the Beatles in July, much to the relief of Paul, who was jealous of Stu's friendship with John, and perhaps even more so over Stu's popularity with their audiences – his rendition of "Love Me Tender" drew greater applause than anything else the band played. Paul took over Stu's bass duties.

Returning to art school, Stu began suffering acute headaches, severe enough to sometimes blind him. In February 1962 he collapsed, and sought treatment back in Britain – but was told by doctors that nothing was wrong.

He collapsed again two months later, on April 10. Astrid, riding in the ambulance on the way to the hospital, held him in her arms – and there he died. He was only 21.

The cause of death was brain hemorrhage following a ruptured aneurysm. The cause of the aneurysm can never be known for certain, but there was speculation that it was the product of a skull fracture he had suffered in a scuffle at a Beatles performance outside Lathom Hall the previous year.

Astrid was inconsolable. Three days after Stu's death, she met John, Paul and Pete at the Hamburg airport and gave them the news. George and manager Brian Epstein arrived shortly thereafter, and John did his best to help – but was likewise overcome with grief, "just crying his eyes out."

Astrid would soon go on to design the Beatles' infamous "mop top" haircut; she would remain a photographer for a while, but would lean away from the craft in the late Sixties.[15] Klaus Voormann would design the cover of *Revolver* in 1966, and three years later become the bassist of John's Plastic Ono Band – then proceeding to play on George's *All Things Must Pass*.

Stu Sutcliffe appears on the cover of *Sgt. Pepper*. Astrid died in May 2020.

And it isn't a stretch to hear both Stu and Astrid in "In My Life", when John sings

Some are dead and some are living
In my life, I've loved them all...

---

[15] Even so, her work would one day be featured in the Rock 'n' Roll Hall of Fame.

Scandal-Worthy

As the Beatles entered Abbey Road studios for the first time in June 1962, preparing to audition for George Martin, they were fast on the way to qualifying as scandal-worthy, by British tabloid standards.

All four Beatles (at this time, this still included Pete Best) had contracted gonorrhea during the preceding weeks in Hamburg. John had returned to find his girlfriend Cynthia with child, and Paul had managed to impregnate his girlfriend, Dot Rhone.

Sorting things out as best he could, Brian Epstein went to work. He arranged for discreet medical treatment of all four Beatles, to deal with the venereal disease. In stoic Britain, especially in the days before the sexual revolution, John contracting a sexually-transmitted disease constituted automatic grounds for divorce – and with a child on the way, such a divorce would have been disastrous for both John and the band.

Wankers

With all the wild oat-sowing and Hamburg prostitutes and willing groupies and women back home pregnant, you wouldn't think the boys would have lacked for sexual release back in those early days.

But Paul, in a 2018 interview with *GQ*, tells it otherwise.

The Fab Four, he revealed, were a band that played together, traveled together, roomed together – and whacked off together.

"Instead of just getting roaring drunk and partying... we were all just in these chairs," he reported, "and the lights were out, and somebody started masturbating, so we all did. But, you know, it was just the kind of thing you didn't think much of. Yeah, it's quite raunchy when you think about it. But it was good harmless fun. It didn't hurt anyone."

Well, they were the Beatles, so they had to add their own unique signature to such events. For instance, just to make it more interesting, someone would frequently objectify some attractive celebrity of the moment in order to stimulate their masturbatory fantasies.

"We were just, *'Brigitte Bardot!''Whoo!'*" McCartney said, "and then everyone would thrash a bit more."

And even that wasn't Beatlesque enough a twist for the ritual. From time to time, John would offer his own singular input:

"Winston Churchill!"

Bye Bye, Heartthrob!

The dismissal of original Beatles drummer Pete Best is well-documented – the result of a growing realization by the rest of the band (which, at the time of that dismissal, consisted of John, Paul, and George, as original bassist Stu Sutcliffe had left the band) that his drumming wasn't up to par with the rest of the band's growing competence.

That realization was bolstered by George Martin's assessment, after the band's EMI audition at Abbey Road on June 6, 1962. The band laid down "Love Me Do", and Martin wasn't happy with Pete's timing.

"I decided that the drums, which are really the backbone of a good rock group, didn't give the boys enough support," he later said. "They needed a good solid beat, and I said to Brian, 'Look, it doesn't matter what you do with the boys, but on record, nobody need know. I'm gonna use a hot drummer.' Brian said, 'Okay, fine.' I felt guilty because I felt maybe I was the catalyst that had changed his life."[16]

But there was more to it: the fact was, Pete was the best-looking Beatle, by a couple of miles. And the rest of them knew it: if any member of the band could be considered a heartthrob by teenage female fan standards, it was Pete.

"The real difference between Ringo Starr and Pete Best was obvious," wrote Lennon biographer Albert Goldman. "Ringo was as homely and uncompetitive as Pete was handsome and self-assured... John Lennon has resented Pete's quiet strength nearly as much as Paul McCartney was jealous of Pete's good looks. Ultimately, the balance of power in the Beatles had to be struck between John and Paul, neither of whom had any use for a third man whose appeal could not be denied or surpassed. Consequently, the odd man out had to get out – and the new man in had to be an odd fellow."

---

[16] In fairness to Pete, Martin had similar misgivings about Ringo.

Beatle biographer Bob Spitz documented just how acute the division between Pete and the others became, where the female fans were concerned:

"[Promoter] Ron Appleby recalled an incident that would soon have far-reaching repercussions. 'Brian Epstein decided that everyone who came to the dance [where the Beatles were playing] before eight o'clock would be given a photograph of the Beatles.' It was a nice incentive, although an unusual practice for a Liverpool dance, and it went over in a big way before taking an unforeseen turn. 'The girls were ripping up the photograph and sticking the picture of Pete Best onto their jumpers.'"

Pete was embarrassed by this, according to Spitz, who quoted Bill Harry: "Almost since he joined the band, Pete was the most popular Beatle. He was certainly the best-looking among them, and the girls used to go bananas over him."

Spitz recorded that local DJ Bob Wooler would introduce the Beatles at Cavern shows, inspiring "an orgasm of shrieks" by announcing *"Mean, moody, and magnificent... Mr. Pete Best!"*

"Paul would seethe as he listened to the swell of female approval, although he didn't need a cheering section to know that he was being overshadowed," Spitz wrote. "To him, the implications were all too clear: if this was allowed to continue unchecked, Pete would wind up the Beatles' heartthrob."

Martin's decision not to use Pete in the studio gave the others an excuse to do what they wanted to do anyway – get a new drummer. All three remaining Beatles, as well as their entourage, would wax eloquent on how Pete simply didn't fit in; he kept to himself, didn't share their sense of humor, through off a loner vibe that didn't mesh well with their own public exuberance. They scoped out the possibility of replacing him with Ringo Starr, who had already sat in with the band a time or two when Pete had been ill, and took their decision to Brian Epstein.

Their manager "was not anxious to change the membership of the Beatles at a time when they were developing as personalities," he wrote in his autobiography, *A Cellarful of Noise*. "I asked the Beatles to leave the group as it was."

They stood firm. Moreover, they farmed out the job of telling Pete he was fired to Epstein himself... an act of no little irony, as

Epstein – a closeted homosexual - saw Pete as more than just a drummer.

Peter Brown, who worked alongside Brian for years, wrote that Epstein's motivations where the Beatles were concerned were certainly erotic. Brown wrote that the Beatles represented a "personification of his secret sexual desires." His primary objective in this domain: to bed Pete.

He made his move, according to Goldman, on a drive to Blackpool one evening, saying, "Pete, would you find it embarrassing if I ask you to stay in a hotel overnight? I'd like to spend the night with you." Pete declined.[17]

Pete was called in by Epstein, then, to find himself ousted – ironically, by the person in the Beatles camp who most wanted him to stay. He was summoned on August 16, and Epstein gave him the heartbreaking news.

The action took Martin by surprise. And in the course of defending his own role in Pete's dismissal, he reiterated Pete's value to the band as eye candy.

"I never suggested that Pete Best must go," he said later. "All I said was that for the purposes of the Beatles' first record I would rather use a sessions man. I never thought that Brian Epstein would let him go. He seemed to be the most saleable commodity as far as looks went."

Reinforcing this perception was the fan reaction. They were subjected to angry protests from female fans, both on the street and when they were on stage: *"Pete forever! Ringo never!"*

Eventually, of course, it all died down, and Ringo was accepted wholeheartedly. And Paul and John got what they wanted: a drummer who fit in perfectly with the band's collective façade, and who was more comic relief than heartthrob – no threat to their dominance. Even so, guilt over what they had done would linger for years, and receive considerable skeptical attention in the many biographies of the band.

---

[17]Pete's account of the exchange is found in his autobiography, *Beatle! The Pete Best Story*. Once Pete was out of the picture, Brian set his sights on John. That story follows.

"We were cowards when we sacked him," John admitted. In more ways than one.

The Pronoun Songs

One of the band's most brilliant moves, right out of the gate, was the tendency of John and Paul to write lyrics that leveraged *pronouns*, words presented in first-person, to create the feeling that *the singer is singing directly to the listener*. When the singer is a world-famous rock star and the listener is a teenager girl in suburban Cincinnati, the effect is electric!

Almost every one of the Beatles' early hit singles (and most of the remaining tracks on their early albums) follow this formula, which they continued to use to some degree until the end. Many reviewers and musical analysts have taken note not only of this technique's ubiquity but also its growing cleverness, as John and Paul found ever-more inventive ways of pronouning their deepening themes.

Initially, the duo's pronouning took the standard form:

I->You, You->Me

...a standard form, used in pop songs for decades, from Elvis Presley's "I Want You, I Need You, I Love You" to Frank Loesser's "I Don't Want to Walk Without You, Baby". The Beatles worked the daylights out of it in their first three years, with either John or Paul singing directly to the girl at the other end of the record player – "Love Me Do", "P.S. I Love You", "From Me to You," "I Want to Hold Your Hand", "I Should Have Known Better", to name but a few. But even at the very beginning, on the title track of the first album, they were innovating:

I->Her, "I->You"

...where John is I and he's speaking to the listener (who *isn't* You) and quotes himself, repeating words he said about Her, who in the quotes becomes You.

Confused yet? This new pattern is a step beyond the album's first track, the seminal "I Saw Her Standing There", which presents the variation

I->You, Her

...as in, Paul is I and the You is not Her, the You is the *listener* and the I is speaking *about* Her. He did it again with "And I Love Her". But even that simple pattern can be well-varied, with "She Loves You", which was brand-spanking new as a pop narrative:

I->(She->You)

...where John and Paul are *both* I, and it isn't either one of them that's into the She – they are cluing the listener in on Her feelings, not for I, but for You. "You're Going to Lose That Girl" took it even further, with I lecturing You that Her won't stand for You much longer – and if You don't straighten up, she's Mine.

See what they did there?

With these newfound powers, there was no stopping them – it became a literary exercise without bound:

I (x)->You, He(y)->You, He(y)->You(z)

...or, in an actual song, I (This Boy) singing words of love to You, and warning You about the dastardly ways of He (That Boy), with the unprecedented innovation of You – the female listener – first appearing in the song in third person (My Girl).

Now *that's* a model worthy of Stephen Hawking.

Several albums in, we begin to see some divergence, with John descending almost monastically into I and Paul cultivating We (usually We was He and Jane Asher)

I->You (We)

He delivered up a wide range of We, generating a veritable guidebook to relationships with these songs alone: "Things We Said Today", "We Can Work It Out", "Why Don't We Do It in the Road?"

John's increasing monasticism surfaced endlessly, usually in the form

I->You(pl), I->Her

...as in "You've Got to Hide Your Love Away", where You is not one listener but *all* listeners (second person plural), an exception being "In My Life",

I->They, I->You

...where the plural is applied to third-person everybody, but You is someone special (second person singular).

At this point, Paul reverts to I->You, You->Me for the most part – "Got to Get You into My Life", "The Long and Winding Road"), slipping occasionally into third-person plural ("She Came in Through the Bathroom Window"), and John would similarly rely on second-person plural ("All You Need is Love").

But they weren't done innovating. Oh, no; John took a mere 15 words, in "I Want You (She's So Heavy)" and constructed not only the group's most sexual song, but an ingenious pronoun fake-out:

I ->You(1), I->You(2), You(1)=She

...with I (John) addressing You (Yoko) in second person, until he turns and addresses the listener, with Yoko becoming She.

And every now and then, they just took the lid off. Take, for instance, "She Said She Said"...

She("I")->"You"(Me), I->"You"(She)

...a pronouning masterpiece, where I is recalling She saying things to I, calling Him You, and vice versa – all the while telling the story to the listener, so that the whole exchange sounds like something happening in a crowded room.

But the final word, ironically, goes to George, who came up with a pronoun model so perfect and intense that it's written into the title of the song:

I Me Mine

"P.S. I Love You"

In their first half-year as recording artists, the Beatles rapidly established themselves in the Love Song domain. "I Saw Her Standing There", "Love Me Do", "Please Please Me" and others not only made clear that they were put on this earth to sing enthusiastically to girls, but that they intended to do so with great creativity and zest.

It is "P.S. I Love You", however, that has the distinction of being the first Beatles song to be about someone real. According to Dot Rhone, that someone was her.

The timeframe fits; written entirely by Paul in 1961, the song is nestled in the second year of their relationship. Moreover, the song is written in the form of a letter – and he made of point of diligently corresponding with Dot while on tour. He acknowledged the format explicitly later in interviews:

"There are certain themes that are easier than others to hang a song on," he said, "and a letter is one of them." He would go on to write more "letter songs," of course; "Paperback Writer" is a blatant example.

The song is gentle and endearing, and the "letter" format makes it all the more intimate:

> *As I write this letter, send my love to you*
> *Remember that I'll always be in love with you*
> *Treasure these few words 'til we're together*
> *Keep all my love forever*
> *P.S. I love you, you, you, you...*
>
> *I'll be coming home again to you, love*
> *And 'til the day I do, love*
> *P.S. I love you, you, you, you*

The lyrical narrative is consistent with the state and routine of the romance in progress between Dot and Paul – a romance tainted behind the scenes by his Hamburg infidelities. All the more motivation to assuage his spirit in song.

The thing is – Paul later denied that the song was written for Dot, claiming it was (like the other Beatles love songs recorded at that point) generic, written for no girl in particular.

Performed in the original EMI audition session in June 1962, it was re-recorded on September 11. In that session, Andy White was drumming (George Martin wasn't yet satisfied with Ringo's playing), and it was decided that drums were too heavy for the song. White played bongos instead, with Ringo adding maracas.

Intended as the B-side of the "Love Me Do" single, the band loved the playback so much that they lobbied for it to take the A-side. They were dissuaded, however, because the song isn't as upbeat as "Love Me Do", and there was already a "P.S. I Love You" out there, written by Johnny Mercer.

A quick survey of the songs preceding it reveals "P.S. I Love You" to be a step forward, for the band as a whole and Paul as a writer. Those earlier songs were very much relationship songs, enthusiastically celebrating the woman in the lyric, and filled with male appeals to the heart; but this song is explicitly about longing, about the yearning that rises up in the mind when separation must be endured.

It's hard to imagine, given all this, that Paul *didn't* write the song for Dot. In the end, we have evidence in both directions – but we will likely never know for certain.

"Can you imagine what it must have been like for her reading in the papers that I didn't know anyone named Maureen Cox?"

~Ringo, referring to his new wife

1963:

I Want to Hold Your Hand

For the Love of Ringo

Once he'd joined the team, Ringo would prove to be as randy and wild-oats as his bandmates, out on the road. At home, however, he was the most steadfast of the bunch: he was utterly committed to Maureen Cox, the teenage girl who would become his wife, and his love for her was real and unequivocal.

She was only 15 in 1961 when she, like so many teenage girls in Liverpool, would queue up in front of the Cavern Club to see the Beatles. And like so many teenage girls in the Cavern, she would try to position herself strategically so that when the Beatles were onstage and rocking, she'd be close enough to the stage to be visible.

But the usually unassuming Maureen found herself growing uncharacteristically bold. One evening, between sets, she walked right up to Paul and kissed him. Not long after, she ran into Ringo randomly outside the Cavern on the street, and kissed him, too, collecting his autograph while she was at it.

And about three weeks after that, when she was at the Cavern listening to another band – probably Ringo's old band, Rory Storm and the Hurricanes – Ringo appeared and asked her to dance.

He escorted her home that night, and they would continue to meet and dance and walk home like that for several weeks, until he finally asked her out.

Their mutual idea of a great date was strolling around the streets of Liverpool, and that one date became many. Maureen called him Richy, and would later describe him as "cheerful" and "peaceful". They rapidly committed to seeing only each other. (She didn't know at the time that this commitment was a bit shaky on his side; he was, at the same time, also seeing model Vicky Hodge.)

As their relationship grew, Maureen was pressured by manager Brian Epstein to remain as far in the background as possible, catering to his conviction that the band would fade away rapidly if the female fans became convinced that each Beatle was spoken for. When journalists would inquire whether a Beatle was seeing this woman or that, the band would deny it; when Maureen was seen with Ringo on tour, she was identified as his secretary.

"Can you imagine," Ringo said later, "what it must have been like for her reading in the papers that I didn't know anyone named Maureen Cox?"

A year passed, and as the Beatles grew in popularity and spent more time abroad on tour, Maureen found herself, along with Cynthia and Dot, the latest member of the Girls Back Home club. Cynthia's memory of Maureen was that she was, in private, not at all the girl in the background she seemed to be in public. Marc Shapiro quoted her: "Far from being a shy little thing, Maureen was talkative, full of laughter and great fun. Maureen was one of the most down to earth, honest people I ever knew."

The relationship was kept under wraps, as all Beatles long-term relationships were, to keep her safe from the wrath of female fans.[18] It wasn't until May of 1963, when she and Ringo took a vacation in Greece with Paul and Jane, that their relationship was publicly acknowledged.

In the press, however, she denied that it was anything serious, that they had any intention of tying the knot. That changed, however, when Ringo collapsed during a photo shoot in 1964 and had to be rushed to the hospital; he had acute tonsillitis and a fever of 103. Maureen moved into his London home and visited him daily, until he was fully recovered – at which point he proposed, and she accepted.

It took her by surprise. "I wasn't trying to take advantage of the situation and I had no idea whether me visiting him would lead to anything more," she later said. "To tell you the truth, the idea of having to move to London permanently was putting me off."

They were married in a small civil ceremony that included John and George (Paul was away) on February 11, 1965 – one month after learning, at age 18, that she was pregnant, making

---

[18] So extreme was this wrath, according to Ringo biographer Michael Seth Starr, that Maureen had to sneak into the back seat of Ringo's car and hide under a blanket before he left the Cavern for the evening, so that he would appear to everyone watching that he was going home alone.

her the third young Liverpool girl to get knocked up by a Beatle.[19] As he had done with John and Cynthia, Brian Epstein swiftly made all the arrangements for the wedding and a covert honeymoon.

Maureen immediately found herself immersed in the more burdensome corner of Beatles life, hounded constantly by journalists and photographs – and irate female fans who felt she'd usurped their destinies. She accepted it all philosophically.

In those earlier years, Maureen saw a very different Ringo in their private moments, a Ringo far afield of the droll clown paraded in the press – someone not unlike John:

"I was finding that he had this real big inferiority complex about him," she said. "He just constantly wanted me to reassure him that I loved him because he gets so afraid. We would be lying in bed and he would hold me close to him and say, 'Do you really love me?' I would constantly have to reassure him that I did. He was just so afraid that I might not love him."

She kept a low profile as they settled into married life, being as domestic as possible. Their son Zak was born in September, and as the touring years ended and the studio years beckoned, the Beatles' drummer took point as the band's only true family man.

---

[19] Peter Brown put it like this: "Like any northern girl, Maureen ensnared her man the northern way; by mid-January she was pregnant. Ringo, like any good northern man, did what was expected."

Jane Asher

Paul first saw Jane Asher, a teenage actress from a respectable London West End family, on the popular BBC program *Juke Box Jury*, which aired on Saturdays. A four-person panel would listen to the latest pop songs, voting each a Hit or a Miss, and one night in 1963 a new panelist appeared – the 16-year-old Jane.

And when the Beatles headlined Swinging Sound '63 soon after, she was assigned to interview them. On that occasion, John made his mission to embarrass her just for the fun of it, and Paul stepped in to spare her, then taking her to a bedroom.

All they did in the bedroom, however, was chat. But it was clear to Paul in that first conversation that he had stumbled something he hadn't realized he'd been searching for in a relationship.

"Jane gave Paul instant access to all the refinement and culture his mother Mary could ever have wished for him," wrote biographer Philip Norman. "They spent their first dates mainly going to the theater, spoilt for choice in the West End that was only a few minutes' walk from Jane's house."

Paul soon moved into a room at the Ashers' Wimpole Street residence, where he got to know her well-to-do but unconventional parents (her father was a maverick physician who had written a number of innovative medical papers) and older brother Peter. Jane's mother made a basement room and piano available for Paul and John to use as a songwriting lair.[20]

Paul was rapidly embraced as one of the family, who took it in stride when the world finally figured out he was in residence on Wimple Street, causing female fans to picket the place. He even wrote a hit song for Peter, "A World Without Love", which he recorded with musical partner Gordon Waller. (It went to #1 in the UK.)

"Paul fell like a ton of bricks for Jane," wrote Cynthia in *A Twist of Lennon*. "The first time I was introduced to her was at her home and she was sitting on Paul's knee. My first impression

[20]They wrote a number of their best works there, including "I Want to Hold Your Hand".

of Jane was how beautiful and finely featured she was. Her mass of Titian-coloured hair cascaded around her face and shoulders, her pale complexion contrasting strongly with dark clothes and shining hair. Paul was obviously as proud as a peacock with new lady. For Paul, Jane Asher was a great prize."

Paul's world would now be filled with the finest music, theater and art that London had to offer – something he hadn't really known he needed. And by his side was a woman worthy of such a lifestyle, raised from birth to appreciate and immerse herself in them.

It would be misleading to suggest that, in partnering with Jane, could be called a social climber. His interest in art and culture for its own sake was as authentic as could be, and his easy way of fitting in to any crowd, regardless of social status, was a consequence of his natural charm. With Jane, he may have hit a jackpot of sorts, but it wasn't by design.

The problem that would soon become apparent was that Paul and Jane were, if anything, too alike: they were both supremely talented, intellectually curious, and – very unfortunately – equally determined to pursue their careers. Jane, it would turn out, was as dedicated to being an actress as Paul was to being a musician.

And for better or worse, her most famous and impactful role would be the Muse of Paul McCartney.

"All My Loving"

If the inspiration of "P.S. I Love You" is ambiguous, the inspiration of "All My Loving" - the third track on *With the Beatles* – certainly is not. Paul wrote it for Jane.

There are conflicting stories (both from Paul) about where it was written – on a tour bus with Roy Orbison, or standing in front of the bathroom mirror, shaving – but either way, it was written as a love poem for his new sweetheart:

"I wrote 'All My Loving' like a piece of poetry and then, I think, I put a song to it later," he said. "It was the first song I ever wrote where I had the words before the music."

Wherever he wrote it, it happened in the late spring of 1963. He had just moved into a room in the Asher family's West End residence in London.

The song oddly (or, perhaps, cleverly) follows up "P.S. I Love You", a letter song, not as a letter song itself but as a song about writing letters. The theme again is the endurance of love during separation, and this time the object of his longing is clear.

Close your eyes and I'll kiss you
Tomorrow I'll miss you
Remember I'll always be true

And then while I'm away,
I'll write home every day
And I'll send all my loving to you...

It lacks the tenderness of "P.S. I Love You", but on the other hand it deftly manages to balance the optimism of young love with the unsettling realities of managing the challenges of a relationship.

"'All My Loving' follows [John's] 'All I've Got to Do' in a revealing way," writes Tim Riley. "John is suffering behind a contended mask; Paul is rallying toward a happy attitude even though he's saying goodbye to his true love. Lennon can sound whiny, whereas McCartney seldom stoops to self-pity... Lennon's two numbers [on side one of *With the Beatles*] project an emotional urgency; he's not just alone, he's self-ensnarled, unable to escape from himself. Paul sounds liberated, free not just from heartache but from insecurity of any kind. In toying with the same possibilities, they wind up sounding even more different than if they had stuck to their own idiosyncrasies."

Recorded during the second *With the Beatles* session on July 30, 1963, "All My Loving" is made all the more exuberant and upbeat by Paul's spirited walking bass line.

John called the song "...a damn good piece of work."

"All My Loving" was also the Beatles' live television introduction to the US; it was the first song in their debut performance on *The Ed Sullivan Show* on February 9, 1964.

And it was, in the most sorrowful of bookendings, the song playing over the sound system at Roosevelt Hospital as John was pronounced dead on December 8, 1980.

John and Brian

Cynthia was not the only one who loved John deeply and was hopeful of intimacy with him. Brian Epstein felt pretty much the same way.

That the Beatles' manager was gay was no big secret, though he somehow managed to convince himself that it was.

The big secret was no secret at all; the sister of Neil Aspinall, the Beatles' driver/roadie/assistant, heard about it from a friend and told her brother, who (of course) already knew. Neil told John that his sister knew. And one night John, high as a kite, let it slip to Brian that Neil knew he was queer. Brian "indignantly stormed out," according to his colleague Peter Brown, and confronted Aspinall.

"Why did you tell them I'm queer?" he demanded to know. "It's a lie!"

"You *are* queer," Neil matter-of-factly responded.

"I am not!"

"Are too!"

Brown wrote that the other Beatles, knowing Brian was gay, didn't mind at all. "We were more confused by it than turned off," he quoted Paul as saying. But that didn't stop them from seizing on it as an opportunity to make fun of Brian behind his back. They rechristened his autobiography *A Cellarful of Noise*, calling it *A Cellarful of Boys* – and had an alternate line for "Baby, you're a rich man, too" - "Baby, you're a rich fag Jew".

Brian's intense denial wasn't just a case of kidding himself; it was a default position in Britain, where homosexuality was still regarded as criminal. This was, after all, the country that had mercilessly crucified its own savior, Alan Turing – world-class codebreaker, winner of World War II, inventor of the digital computer – by chemically neutering him and driving him to suicide. Brian could not imagine that his homosexuality was obvious to the most casual observer; but even if he could, he dared not let any such rumor proliferate.

The Beatles not only knew he was gay; they were very clear that he was in love with John. Most of the Beatles entourage were very clear on it.

"[John] was the light of Brian's life and in some small way the impetus for almost everything that Brian did for the Beatles," wrote Brown.

Bob Spitz quoted Brown: "John wasn't a pretty boy, he had a good look, and a general fuck-you attitude, which was a turn on. Once Brian saw John, there was no turning away."

"He was dazzled by John, by his looks, by his wit, even by his cruelty," Brown wrote. "When John spoke, Brian looked away, not daring to gaze directly into his eyes lest his lovesick look expose what he thought was his secret. John was sardonically amused at the power he had over Brian and didn't hesitate to use it to be manipulative or mean. This, in turn, fueled Brian's masochism and made him desire John even more."

John, for his part, wasn't trying to lead Brian on, but he did spend more time with him than the others did – not out of affection or physical attraction, but in order to secure his position as the band's leader. This included accompanying Brian to underground gay clubs, where John would observe from the sidelines with amusement, but would not join in. This had to be an encouragement to Brian that his desire for John was not in vain.

He made a standing offer to John to take him to Copenhagen for the weekend, anytime John felt like getting out of town.

In 1988, Albert Goldman asserted in his Lennon biography, *The Lives of John Lennon*, very controversially, that Brian eventually succeeded.

"He and Brian had sex," he wrote. "Naturally John was not eager to avow this fact or to explain his motive, but when challenged by Pete Shotton, John came up with an explanation that echoed the line he had taken up with Cynthia: 'Eppy just kept on and on at me, until one night I just pulled me trousers down and said to him: 'Oh, for Christ's sake, Brian, just stick it up me fucking arse, then.' And he said to me, 'Actually, John, I don't do that kind of thing. That's not what I like to do. 'Well,' I said, 'what is it you like to do, then?' And he said, 'I'd really just like to touch you, John.' And so I left him toss me off."

Goldman was eviscerated by the rock press and Beatles fans all over the world for making such a heretical assertion. Bono of U2 even denounced Goldman in a U2 song - "God, Part II", written as a sequel to John's own song "God": *Don't believe in Goldman / His type like a curse / Instant karma's going to get him / If I don't get him first.* No one wanted to believe that John had actually had sex with Brian.[21]

The thing is, the quoted exchange really did come from Pete Shotton's own memoir, *John Lennon In My Life*. And Pete was, of course, John's oldest and best childhood friend, in whom he confided all his life.

And Shotton had his own Brian story to tell. In the early days of Brian's management of the Beatles, he'd approached Pete in a club where he'd been drinking with John, who got up and left. Brian suggested they take a ride in Brian's Mark 10 Jaguar, where he invited Pete to his apartment.

"What for?" Shotton asked.

"I think you know what for," Brian replied, giving him a strange look.

"No, no, Brian," Shotton replied. "That's not my scene."

"Oh, all right, then, Pete," Brian said offhandedly. "No problem. I do hope I haven't offended you."

"No offense taken," Shotton answered. "Actually, I take it as a compliment!"

The night Pete described that he and Goldman reported in their books occurred in April 1963 in Barcelona, Spain.[22]

As John's confidante Pete Shotton's report supported Goldman's assertion, so did Peter Brown's - and Brown had a similar place in Epstein's life. His version:

---

[21] Goldman's biography of John was criticized for more than just his documentation of John's relationship with Brian; it also claimed he had solicited underage male prostitutes in Thailand, among other things. It is well-deserving of the harsh criticism it has received – but not for what it says about the events described here.

[22] A fictionalized film account of John and Brian's Barcelona weekend, *The Hours and Times*, was released in 1991.

"...back in their hotel suite, drunk and sleepy from the sweet Spanish wine, Brian and John undressed in silence. 'It's okay, Eppy,' John said, and lay down on the bed. Brian would have liked to have hugged him, but he was afraid. Instead, John lay there, tentative and still, and Brian fulfilled the fantasies he was so sure would bring him contentment, only to awake the next morning as hollow as before."

John referenced the whole thing circumspectly 17 years later, in a 1980 *Playboy* interview not long before his death:

"Well, it was almost a love affair, but not quite," he said. "It was never consummated... but we did have a pretty intense relationship."

Cynthia is on record stating that she believed that John's relationship with Brian was always platonic. But neither she nor the other Beatles doubted Brian's feelings.

"I'm sure Brian was in love with John," Paul said in *The Beatles Anthology*. "We were all in love with John, but Brian was gay so that added an edge."

What does any of this matter?

For a start, look at how completely pulled out of the present we are by this question of John and Brian (and have been, steadily, since the Sixties). If John or any other Beatle had been gay or bisexual – *so what???* Today, we wouldn't give this a second thought; endless are the bands that have emerged since the Beatles that have had LGBTQ members, and no one thinks twice. Even Judas Priest's Rob Halford's coming-out scarcely created a ripple; Styx bassist Chuck Panozzo's HIV and subsequent AIDS awareness and gay rights campaigns are, today, an on-going inspiration.

So what if a Beatle had sex with a man?

We *are* pulled out of the present by this, and that serves to remind us just how far we've come. Queen Elizabeth apologized, on behalf of Britain, to the ghost of Alan Turing in 2013. The fact that we've come so far since the days when a Brian Epstein could live such a tortured life and a John Lennon could be so jaw-droppingly fossilized in the world's pious expectations and an Albert Goldman could be so vehemently denounced just for quoting John and Brian's closest friends, is a testimony to the fact that we've lived through a magnificent revolution in the intervening decades.

And who, exactly, gave us that revolution? Who, exactly, shattered every trope and cliché in pop culture about love and relationships? Who, exactly, showed us it's okay to explore our sexuality honestly and express our insecurities?

Who, exactly, reminded us that all we need is love?

"I think I had my first orgasm at a Beatles Concert - then again, how would I have known? When you're preteen, prepubescent and pretty much pre-everything, 'I Want to Hold Your Hand' seems the height of erotic ambition. And that was especially true in 1964, before the sexual revolution and the Internet made that kind of ignorance unimaginable."

~Jeanette Catsoulis

1964:

With a Love Like That, You Know You Should Be Glad

Satyricon

If free sex had become a tsunami when the band had crossed the channel to Hamburg, it was an unstoppable hurricane once they began touring the world.

"Sex had always been pressingly on offer," wrote Philip Norman, "whether on the Reeperbahn or outside the Cavern, when roadie Neil Aspinall and his hulking deputy, Mal Evans, would bring in willing females along with the takeaway fish and chips or chicken. After Brian arrived and the world touring began, it became part or room service. Among the Beatles' welcoming delegation at airports across America would usually be four high-priced, prepaid hookers to console them for being unable to set foot outside their hotels.

"Not that it ever needed to be a commercial transaction, especially not for Paul. In any room he entered, he knew he could have his pick of the most beautiful young women there. During early Beatlemania, he would often as act as a judge at bathing beauty contests – as yet unchallenged by feminism – whose winners might then receive an extra prize along with a crown, a sash and a bouquet of roses."

Group activity was not out of bounds, however:

"Pop musicians with wives or steady girlfriends observed an unwritten rule that 'sex on tour doesn't count', but for Paul is was more often a matter of keeping count," wrote Philip Norman. "To his cousin, Mike Robbins, he once described a four-in-a-bed session in which he'd been the only male. The holiday camps where Robbins once worked used to be saturated in sex, but even he had to admit Butlin's had nothing on this."

Paul kindasorta almost denied it:

"There weren't really orgies, to my knowledge," he told *GQ*. "There were sexual encounters of the celestial kind, and there were groupies. The nearest it got... See, this is my experience, because I'm just not into orgies. I don't want anyone else there, personally. It ruins it! I would think - I've never actually done it. Didn't appeal to me, the idea. There *was* once when we were in Vegas where the tour guy, a fixer, said, 'You're going to Vegas, guys - you want a hooker?' We were all, 'Yeah!' And I requested two. And I had them, and it was a *wonderful* experience. But that's the closest I ever came to an orgy. See, the thing is, in the next room I think the guys might have ordered something else off the menu. So that would figure if John was saying, yeah, it was all bacchanalian. I think John was a little more that way, because thinking back, I remember there was someone in a club that he'd met, and they'd gone back to the house because the wife fancied John, wanted to have sex with him, so that happened, and John discovered the husband was watching. That was called 'kinky' in those days."

The press willingly colluded in all of this; the objects of their professional attention were, after all, considered cultural treasures, and they were not about to sully their images.

"The Beatles on-the-road sexual activities were well-known to the large media contingent who traveled with them, at close quarters that today seem extraordinary," Norman wrote. "But no newspaper or TV reporter would have dreamed of dishing the dirt on the sacred Fab Four, any more than of delving into their murky Hamburg past. The media were as complicit in preserving the illusion as White House correspondents during the presidency of John F. Kennedy."

John would later confirm that the reality of touring life had been white-washed by the press: "There was nothing about orgies and the shit that happened on tour.... The Beatles tours were like the Fellini film *Satyricon*."

And sometimes these transactions happened out in the open: "...In Atlantic City, at a motel party following the concert at Convention Hall, the girls on call were too spectacular to resist," according to Bob Spitz. "John, especially, couldn't take his eyes off a slim and flashy young blonde who 'reminded him of Brigette Bardot.' And again, in Dallas, when bunnies from a private club showed up, the boys yielded to temptation. This time it was Paul who fancied a tall blond cowgirl standing somewhat behind the others. Art Schreiber, who happened to be passing through the suite, was startled when Paul motioned with his chin and whispered, 'I like that one. Can you get her for me?'

Answered Schreiber: 'Listen, pal, I'm no fucking pimp. I'm a reporter."

Pattie Boyd

Pattie Boyd is distinct in the Beatles story in several ways. First and foremost, she wasn't a Liverpool girl.

Where Cynthia, Dot, and Maureen were all from the working-class town by the sea, Pattie was a wartime baby in a military family that moved from one country to another throughout her youth. She returned to England with her mother just before reaching her teens after her parents divorced.

A staggering blonde beauty, Pattie began to get modeling jobs in London and Paris in the early Sixties, and found herself in demand, requiring an agent to coordinate her work. That agent got her some work doing television commercials – in particular, for a director named Richard Lester.

When Lester was casting *A Hard Day's Night*, he remembered the beautiful blonde he'd used in a commercial for Smith's Crisps and called her agent. Pattie found herself on the set of the first Beatles film.

Her part was strictly a walk-on, one of several schoolgirls. She and several other actresses met the Beatles on set, and she met George, whom she found "unbelievably good-looking and adorable."

She sat with him at lunch that day, "feeling so silly because I was still dressed in a stupid schoolgirl uniform. We were both really shy but we enjoyed sitting next to each other and talking a bit. Being close to him was electrifying."[23]

At the end of the day's shooting, on the train back to London, "George looked at me and said, 'Will you marry me?' I just laughed as if he were joking. Then he said, 'Can I take you out to dinner tonight?' Then I said, 'Well, actually I'm going out with my boyfriend, but you can come along, too.' He said, 'No, that wasn't the idea at all.'"

She promptly broke up with that boyfriend, photographer Eric Swayne, and made her availability clear to George upon

---

[23]In Shapiro's *Beatle Wives*.

returning to the set several days later. A dinner date was set. Brian Epstein went on the date with them.

Then there was another date, and another, and before long Pattie took her place alongside Cynthia, Maureen and Jane among the Beatle Women.

Pattie found Cynthia to be personable but hard to get to know, because she seemed so "serious"; Maureen was easier for her to be around, "more relaxed." Jane was more her speed; she was a fellow actress, and like Pattie, privately educated.

There was backlash, as usual, from female fans, and George had to go to the extreme of moving from his home to escape them, buying a new one in Surrey, where Pattie lived with him. He had repeated his marriage proposal several times; but Pattie, who had lived through her parents' divorce, was wary.

Finally, in December 1965, she said Yes. Once again, Brian denied a Beatle bride the wedding of her dreams by arranging a quiet and unobtrusive civil ceremony. This time, Paul was the only other Beatle to attend.

"I had always thought I'd have a big white wedding, as all little girls do, then have children and live happily ever after," she wrote in her autobiography. "But I was so happy and so much in love, I didn't care."

On that day – January 21, 1966 – George became the third Beatle husband, and the first Beatle who had become engaged unencumbered by an unexpected pregnancy. This would become ironic later on.

"And I Love Her"

Paul has called "And I Love Her", the next song he wrote with Jane in mind, "the first ballad I impressed myself with." It's easy to see why; it has every element of a top-drawer standard, and represented giant leaps in both his craftsmanship and clarity of emotional expression.

The song itself, composed in the music room of the Asher home sometime in late 1963-early 1964, is deceptively simple: three brief stanzas and a bridge. Within them, Paul professes his undying love, metaphorically declaring it as eternal as the stars:

Bright are the stars that shine
Dark is the sky
I know this love of mine
Will never die
And I love her...

The music on its face is as simple as the lyrics, but upon examination shows unprecedented sophistication. It is intentionally somber in tone, eschewing the ebullience of previous Beatles work: Paul was shooting for a song that would, frankly, transcend the band; he wanted to join the pantheon of songwriters who had built out popular music in the Twenties and Thirties – his father's era.

And he did it. "And I Love Her" is no I-IV-V pop knock-off.

The song opens with simple Latin percussion under George's four-note riff, hovering between the related keys of C#m and E. The verses remain in the minor key through Paul's impassioned declarations, settling back to the smiling E chord at the end of each phrase, as he declares "...and I love her." It's marvelously effective, giving the song real gravity without rendering it morose.

After the third verse has passed, the heart is stirred yet again with a sudden modulation to the key of F, as George recapitulates the melody in his solo. Paul follows immediately with a repeat of the third verse (the starry one), underscoring his metaphor of vast, infinite love. The opening riff is repeated – and the song leaps yet again, finishing on a transcendent D major chord (a Picardy Third, perfectly executed).

The band's all-acoustic rendering (a Beatles first), with Ringo on bongos and George adding claves, gives the song the feel of a Latin love song, complete with moonlight. Even George's solo, performed on classical guitar, evokes the feel of stargazing from a balcony.

As he did with "P.S. I Love You" and Dot Rhone, Paul stated many years later that the song was not, in fact, inspired by Jane – a claim that is even harder to accept than the earlier one.

It's hard to know what to make of this. Paul is clearly growing as a songwriter here, learning how to express his feelings openly and without artifice, embracing over-the-top self-expression without descending into cliché. The sheer economy and brilliant structure of the song speak to songcraft that is blossoming almost exponentially. He's shooting for the stars – but do we just buy into the idea that he just wants to be Cole Porter?

"With one stroke, [Paul] gains the status of standard balladeer composer that he strived toward as early as 'P.S. I Love You'," wrote Tim Riley. "The haunting melody is dressed up with tasteful acoustic guitar playing, a subtle percussive line, and a deft key change for George's classical guitar solo to keep the ear interested in what would otherwise be a repetition of a simple musical idea. For the final chord, the minor tonality inverts to major.

"The tension between the lyrics and the melody bears some similarity to the irony of 'All My Loving' - the melody alone doesn't suggest such positive words. Paul sings it with melancholy against George's high guitar arpeggios that hover over the last verse. If these moon-in-June lyrics had been set in more ordinary fashion, the song would be dismissible. But considered by itself, this tune is among the best Paul will ever write, imbuing the cliché lyrics with a plaintive undertow. The tug between the two gives the song substance: the music underscores his loyalty with an utterable sorrow."

The band recorded it on February 25-27, 1964. John, who helped Paul write the song's bridge, would later call it "Paul's first 'Yesterday'".

From Me to You: John and Cyn

It is unsurprising that songwriters of the Beatles caliber not only routinely mined their own experiences for inspiration, but used their songs to communicate to others in their lives. This is, after all, an established standard operating procedure in pop/rock, country, and most any genre you can think of.

So it was with the three Beatle songwriters. Each of them wrote songs either about the woman in their lives, or directly *to* her, expressing some thought or emotion that in lesser hands might have found itself conveyed through a Hallmark card.

Some very famous examples will follow. But even the least among these entries has something to say about the sort of young men the Beatles were.

John, for instance, was both the first Beatle to marry and the first to become a father (though it briefly appeared as though Paul was trying to beat him out on the latter). It was a marriage of necessity, not love, and so he didn't really write a song for Cynthia that he ever acknowledged (though there has been speculation for decades that several of the earliest Beatles hits written by him were inspired by her, including "Ask Me Why", "All I've Got to Do", "You Can't Do That" and "When I Get Home").

He did, however, acknowledge her inspiration of at least a piece of a song – long after they were together, and more than a year after their divorce.

"I was lying next to my first wife in bed, you know, and I was irritated, and I was thinking. She must have been going on and on about something and she'd gone to sleep and I kept hearing these words over and over, flowing like an endless stream. I went downstairs and it turned into a sort of cosmic song rather than an irritated song, rather than a 'Why are you always mouthing off at me?'"

The line?

Words are flowing out like endless rain into a paper cup
They slither wildly as they slip away across the universe...

"If I Fell"

It's easy to hear "If I Fell" as John's attempt to answer Paul's "And I Love Her" with something tender and endearing of his own. Tender, it certainly sounds; the dual vocal lines mesh so perfectly – breathtakingly beautiful! - that the listener would swoon to them even if the words were gibberish. John considered his effort a success on those terms, calling it his first "proper ballad."[24] He also said it was a precursor to "In My Life".

Tender, yes; endearing, the song certainly is not. Paul's love songs to this point had been brimming with earnestness and devotion; this, John's first real excursion into balladry, is an almost embarrassing glimpse into a boy who isn't yet a man.

The song, which John would later confess to be "semi-autobiographical," is a me-to-you song from a man who is questioning whether to leave the woman he's with in order to be with the woman he's singing to: *Should I leave her for you?*

If I give my heart
To you
I must be sure
From the very start
That you
Would love me more than her

As gentle and tender as the song presents, it nonetheless becomes something appalling when these lyrics are fully digested. Bad enough that the entire point of the song is the entertainment of infidelity or abandonment; it is furthermore a deeply revealing confession of insecurity and cowardice. He is almost obsessively seeking assurances from the woman that any move he makes away from his current relationship will be as risk-free as possible.

---

[24]Tim Riley: "Breaking up lines with these harmony patterns only increases the temperamental dividends of McCartney singing atop Lennon: John sounds hurt, uneasy but still hopeful; Paul is romantic, yearning, and full of promise. Their vocal blend conveys the emotional quandary."

So openly does John convey his ambivalence that it is reflected in his composition:

"In the introduction of the song 'If I Fell', very unusual to have an E flat minor go to a D major chord to a D flat major chord. Very, very strange progression – and yet it makes all the sense in the world if you're trying to get across the idea of being tentative, not being sure you want to enter a relationship. It's the perfect musical analog to that feeling of holding back, and it's not goal-directed. It's very ambiguous and loose, and it makes sense. And it's probably a progression Paul McCartney would not have written."

Ian Macdonald analyzed the sentiment of the song, delivering an appropriate final verdict:

"Lennon... later recalled this as his first shot at a ballad, comparing it harmonically with 'In My Life' and hinting at similar personal content. This casts a different light on the song, in particular the plea in its second line which anticipates the more desperate 'Help!' by over a year. But if the young Lennon's fear of seeming 'soft' fits the pained hesitance of 'If I Fell', its almost demure embarrassment is too immature for a man of 23 with five orgiastic years on the road behind him."

Put another way: while "If I Fell" was unquestionably a major step forward for John from the standpoint of songcraft, its content is a blinking neon sign that broadcasts his lack of development as a man, for all the world to see.

The Beatles recorded the song on February 27, 1964. Intended for the film *A Hard Day's Night*, it found itself with nowhere to go, and in the movie John sings the song to Ringo (we'll steer clear of analyzing that).

Lennon biographer Philip Norman called it "a plaintive John ballad that made grannies go gooey long before anything of Paul's."

Ironically, John scribbled the first draft of the lyrics on the back of a Valentine's Day card.

"Will you marry me? Well, if you won't marry me, will you have dinner with me tonight?"

~George to Pattie Boyd, on the set of *A Hard Day's Night*

The Beatles Guide to Love & Sex

1965:

I Think I'm Gonna Be Sad

"Ticket to Ride"

Already well on his way to being the poster boy for young male insecurity, John threw down with what might be considered the first true heavy metal song ever recorded: "Ticket to Ride", the band's first UK single of 1965.

Paul claimed to have contributed to the writing, but John insisted that the song was entirely his, and that Paul's contribution was limited to suggesting Ringo's innovative drum pattern when the song was recorded. John also gave multiple descriptions of the song's origins, eventually settling on a recollection that the prostitutes they'd patronized in their Hamburg days were given certification cards that they were STD-free – a "ticket to ride."

This condescending explanation adds nothing whatsoever to the song itself, in which the singer is loudly lamenting the departure of his woman, whose indifferent rejection is tearing him to pieces. It's easy to suppose that John experienced such rejections – but certainly not from the woman he lived with. The song, therefore, is largely fantasy.

I think I'm gonna be sad, I think it's today, yeah
The girl that's driving me mad is going away

John opens with self-pity, proceeding to immediately disclose the sheer intensity of his anxiety. He proceeds to pick at his departing lover's complaints:

She said that living with me is bringing her down, yeah
She would never be free when I was around

He is also stung by her indifference:

She's got a ticket to ride, but she don't care

In speaking of the song years later, John focused on the music, not the lyric, apart from the story he tells above:

"It was [a] slightly new sound at the time, because it was pretty fuckin' heavy for then. If you go and look in the charts for what other music people were making, and you hear it now, it doesn't sound too bad. It's all happening, it's a heavy record."

Ian Macdonald, however, takes the lyrics very seriously, describing it as "psychologically deeper than anything the Beatles had recorded before and a sharp anomaly in a pop scene where doomy melodramas from balladeers like Gene Pitney P.J. Proby stood in for real feeling.

"Though it had appeared in half a dozen Beatles songs, the word 'sad' here carries a weight graphically embodied in the track's oppressive pedal tonality and deliberately cumbersome drums. There is, too, a narcotic passivity about Lennon's lyric: though the girl is leaving him, he makes no attempt to stop or threaten her as he would have done in earlier songs; all he does – in the ruminative, monochordal middle eight – is mutter bitterly while she 'rides high', absorbed in herself (a self whose chief characteristic is that of not caring)."

Kenneth Womack's reading unveils a dark, manipulative interpretation:

"The speaker tries every angle that he can imagine in order to cleave her to him, to win her love, and, at the very least, bargain for sex. When the speaker's threat fall on deaf ears - 'She ought to think twice, she ought to do right by me' - he resorts to the time-honored cheap trick of earning her sympathy by confessing his sadness, his sensitivity. Neither method succeeds, of course, and the music's tension fittingly never ebbs – seeming, instead, to increase as the guitars grow faster, more urgent and destructive, as the speaker repeats 'My baby don't care' with no relief in sight."

Macdonald goes on to credit the tone of both the lyrics and the music to John's new acquaintance with LSD, which he and George had recently discovered:

"This self-centered, addictive outlook, which eventually led him to heroin, is vividly prefigured in the droning sound and lethargic mood of 'Ticket to Ride'."

The band recorded the song on February 15, 1965, as part of the *Help!* Soundtrack.

"You've Got to Hide Your Love Away"

Famously described by John as his attempt to ape Bob Dylan, "You've Got to Hide Your Love Away" is a welcome departure from the insecure, anxiety-ridden screeds he'd been cranking out for years.

On its face, this song puts forth as much insecurity and anxiety as any of its predecessors. But his subject here is veiled, and he's not really writing in the way he had been before. There is depth here; he's not just venting his emotions, he's actually trying to process them.

The song may refer to the frustration he had been experiencing in being forced to keep his marriage a secret from the public; it may also have referred to the oppressive pressure of fame, with which he was never able to truly cope.

The most compelling interpretation, however, came from British singer-songwriter and gay rights activist Tom Robinson, who felt the song, despite its references to an anonymous "she", was really John's expression of empathy for Brian Epstein, whose homosexuality had to be kept secret due to its criminality in Britain.

There's real despair going on here:

Here I stand, head in hand
Turn my face to the wall
If she's gone, I can't go on
Feeling two-foot small

How could she say to me
Love will find a way
Gather round, all you clowns
Let me hear you say...

A deep sense of hopelessness emerges, punctuated by resignation, as he barks a Dylan-esque "Hey!" before delivering the chorus lyric – simply the song's title.

Tim Riley finds the Dylan comparison revealing:

"It's hard to imagine the master of deceit [Dylan] singing so direct a sentiment with such clear, distilled imagery," he wrote. "Although Lennon's delivery here is detached and somewhat restrained, it's still more personally revealing than the masks Dylan wears."

"Feeling two-foot small" was Paul's contribution, in a way; John mistakenly sang *small* when he meant *tall* in playing the song for his partner, and Paul liked it so much that he insisted John keep it in.[25]

The song was recorded by the band for the *Help!* soundtrack on February 18, 1965. Tenor and alto flutes were added by John Scott in the song's coda, to heighten its melancholy.

---

[25]John would return the favor when Paul was writing "Hey Jude", as he dismissed his filler lyric "the movement you need is on your shoulder", which John felt wasn't filler at all – but a perfect expression of the song's message.

Papa Paul

Paternity suits are certainly not uncommon among rock stars, but Paul seems to have had more than his share. Particularly difficult was the case of Bettina Hubers, who, having along with her mother sued Paul repeatedly over the years, alleging his paternity, then accused him of faking the 1983 paternity test that exonerated him of fathering her in 1962. Her long-standing claim is that Paul impregnated her mother Erica during the Beatles' Hamburg days.

Erica successfully sued for support in 1966, and Paul paid, despite denying paternity. In 1983 Bettina sued, and a blood test was done which indicated Paul was *not* her father. Her claim that a right-handed double stood in for him when the blood test was done has not yet resulted in a subsequent test, though a German prosecutor has undertaken an investigation.

Philip Paul Cochrane, born in Liverpool in 1964 to teenager Anita Cochrane, is also alleged to be Paul progeny. In July of that year, Anita's uncle showed up at the Liverpool premiere of *A Hard Day's Night* and distributed hundreds of postcards declaring that McCartney had gotten his niece pregnant, prompting Brian Epstein to provide Anita with money to buy a baby carriage. As an adult, Philip has sold his story to numerous tabloids in both the US and Britain.

"Help!"

John said many, many times that "Help!" was exactly what it purported to be: his personal cry for just that.

"Looking back on this song in 1980," wrote Ian Macdonald, "Lennon recalled it as a cry for help from the depths of what he referred to as his 'Fat Elvis' period. Mentally exhausted by two years of continuous touring, he was isolated and alienated in his multi-roomed mansion in the stockbroker belt of London's western fringe. His marriage damaged by his orgiastic round of whores and groupies on the road, he felt unsustained by his faithful and attentive wife of Cynthia, who, concerned for her husband's health, made no secret of disapproving his drug intake. All of this amounted to a personal malaise that would expand to overwhelming dimensions over the next two years."

John's own analysis was far less nuanced: "I needed the help," he said simply. "The song was about me." The song was written to order for the movie of the same name, it's true; and he did write it with Paul, but the latter's contribution was mainly the marvelous vocal counterpoint in the verses that anticipate the lyrical statements John had already concocted.

He elaborated just a bit: "I just wrote the song because I was commissioned to write it for the movie," he said, "but later, I knew I really was crying out for help... I was fat and depressed and I *was* crying for help."

He originally conceived the song as slower than it turned out, and was mildly resentful when the decision was made during its recording to speed it up and make it more commercial-sounding, as "Please Please Me" had been. "Rather fittingly, the tempo shift serves to underscore the speaker's growing desperation," wrote Kenneth Womack.

"Lyrically, 'Help!' distills Lennon's misery, marking a watershed in his life," Macdonald went on. "Here, the shell he had grown around his feelings since his mother's death finally cracks as he admits a need for others."

"As a knowing study of the human condition, 'Help!' explores the manner in which people carry the potential for evolving into pseudo-selves, or those individuals, according to psychotherapists Charles P. Barnard and Ramon Garrido Corrales, who remain unable to maintain any real stasis between their inner feelings and their outer behavior," Womack wrote. "The song's musical phrasings contributes to the band's unnerving depiction of the speaker's malaise. As Tim Riley observes, 'Since Paul and George anticipate nearly every line Lennon sings in the verse [in the melodic counterpoint], the effect is of voices inside the same head, prodding, goading [the listener] to chilling consequences. By the time Lennon sings "open up the doors," the voices are completely caught up in the nightmare.' Although the speaker in 'Help!' is pointedly reaching out for support, the song offers little in the way of genuine comfort or hope. Instead, he can only contemplate a distant past in which he was allegedly more happy, more secure."

Recorded April 23, 1965, "Help!" not only introduced the Beatles' second feature film, but became its 10th #1 single. It was ranked at #29 in *Rolling Stone*'s 500 Greatest Songs of All Time in 2004 and 2010.

"Yesterday"

Up to this point, Paul's love songs focused on longing, devotion and anticipation, while John's were mostly confessions and reactions to being dumped. Now here comes Paul, with his own song about being dumped, and it is not only an instant classic; it's *the* classic love ballad of the 20th century, one of the greatest songs of all time.

Music aside, we call look at the lyrics of Paul's "Yesterday" and John's "Ticket to Ride" and not only see that they are two songs about exactly the same thing – being dumped - but examine in high relief how the two Beatles differed in their emotional processing of such events.

Above, we note that John's prevailing emotion as "the girl that's driving [him] mad is going away" is self-pity; his focus isn't on what caused the problem, but how it's affecting him. "Ticket to Ride" is more indignation than anything else.

Paul, in lamenting a lost love, is likewise focused on loss, but his emotional response isn't to feel sorry for himself or get indignant; he conveys genuine sorrow:

Suddenly
I'm not half the man I used to be
There's a shadow hanging over me
Oh, yesterday came suddenly...

And his focus goes beyond his emotional reaction to his loss; he ponders what could have happened to bring it about:

Why she had to go, I don't know,
She wouldn't say
I said something wrong,
Now I long for yesterday...

Paul's emotional depth also manages to convey genuine regret, for not fully treasuring what he had, when he had it (The best John can do is petulance, chanting "My baby don't care!" over and over).

Yesterday
Love was such an easy game to play
Now I need a place to hide away
Oh, I believe in yesterday...

Composed and recorded during the *Help!* cinematic adventure, "Yesterday" began as a melody that Paul literally dreamed, emerging completely. He famously spent months trying to write a lyric to match the quality of the composition, which was so good that he couldn't quite believe it had come out of his own head: he asked everyone he knew whether they'd heard it before.

He came up with a filler lyric - "Scrambled Eggs" - and eventually finished off the song.

Once the lyrics did arrive, the union of the music to the words elevated "Yesterday" to "a true masterwork of musical unity, given the exquisite parallelism of the composition's words and music," per Kenneth Womack. Musicologist WilfridMellers elaborated:

"Paul has lost his girl, and although the opening *words* tell us that yesterday his troubles seemed far away, the *music* in the second bar immediately enacts these troubles with a disquieting modulation from tonic, by way of [C#], to the [submediant]. The first bar, with its gentle sigh, seems separated, stranded, by the abrupt modulation; and although the troubles 'return to stay' with a descent to the tonic, the anticipated modulation sharpwards is counteracted when the B natural is flattened to make an irresolute plagal cadence. The 'lost' feeling is incarnate in the irregular phrasing: for that one isolated bar is followed by two, and then by two plus two. This makes seven, leaving us one bar short; but this first irregular strain is completed by the tune's continuation after the double bar: which also, of course, initiates the middle section."

After "Yesterday", the Beatles would never be the same. It started them down a new path, one that was to produce the attributes that would later coalesce into progressive rock. Two of those attributes first appeared in Paul's most beautiful ballad.

"That was when, as I can see it in retrospect, I started to leave my hallmark on the music, when a style started to emerge which was partly of my making," said George Martin in his memoir. "It was on 'Yesterday' that I started to score their music. It was on 'Yesterday' that we first used instruments other than the Beatles and myself. On 'Yesterday', the added ingredient was no more nor less than a string quartet; and that, in the pop world of those days, was quite a step to take. It was with 'Yesterday' that we started breaking out of the phase of using just the four instruments and went into something more experimental, though our initial experiments were severely limited by the fairly crude tools at our disposal, and had simply to be molded out of my recording experience."

Released in the US as a single, it became their 11th #1. There was talk of releasing it as a solo record, credited to Paul alone. Brian Epstein, the band's manager, would have no part of that: "No, whatever we do, we are not splitting up the Beatles!"

On June 14, 1965, "Yesterday" was recorded at Abbey Road. At first, it was attempted as a band number, with John playing organ, but this was quickly abandoned. Producer George Martin suggested that Paul perform the song alone on guitar, and that a string quartet be dubbed later (Paul initially cringed at this suggestion, according to Beatles biographer Bob Spitz: "Oh, no, George. We are a rock 'n' roll band, and I don't think it's a good idea.").

He relented, however, and in fact helped Martin with the score, pushing the producer to break some classical composition rules – the cello's E♭ in the second bridge forms a 7th of the tonic. This musical indiscretion is one of the signature attributes of the song.

Two takes of Paul and his guitar were recorded, with the second deemed best. In the first take, Paul accidentally reversed the lines *I'm not half the man I used to be / There's a shadow hanging over me*, and he can be heard stifling laughter at the flub.

The strings were dubbed three days later, and Paul did an additional vocal, doubling his voice in places. When the strings were recorded, they used vibrato, but Paul insisted – over Martin's objection – that the dub be redone without vibrato.

The final result is gorgeous, especially considering the lack of clean separation: "Paul played his guitar and sang it live, a mic on the guitar and mic on the voice," Martin recalled. "But, of course, the voice comes on to the guitar mic and the guitar comes on to the voice mic. So there's leakage there. Then I said I'd do a string quartet. The musicians objected to playing with headphones, so I gave them Paul's voice and guitar on two speakers either side of their microphones. So there's leakage of Paul's guitar and voice on the string tracks."

Paul recorded the vocals for "Yesterday", "I've Just Seen a Face" and "I'm Down" all on the same day.

The use of the string quartet, to which Paul was originally opposed, is the clear point of demarcation between the Beatles' mop top years and their journey into true musicianship. This transition convinced them – and, for that matter, the rest of the world – that rock wasn't just ritual dance music, but a landscape of endless possibilities.

They would continue to make use not only of classical instrumentation but classical forms, and progressive rock would later do the same. Bands like the Moody Blues, ProcolHarum, Yes, and the Nice (where Keith Emerson spent his salad days) would all make use of orchestral instrumentation, and in fact there is a subgenre within progressive music called *symphonic rock*.

"Yesterday", of course, went on to become the most covered song of all time (the count is now over 3,000), and with seven million radio plays, the all-time airplay leader until "You've Lost That Lovin' Feeling" unseated it in 1999.

"With 'Yesterday', the Beatles had suddenly alighted on a much wider international stage that had granted them an audience of all ages *for the ages*," wrote Kenneth Womack. "In this way, Paul's masterpiece of sorrow and simplicity would radically transform the nature and direction of the band's career. The dye had been once and truly cast, and for Lennon and McCartney, the days of 'She Loves You' were over for good."

The Women of *Rubber Soul*

Rubber Soul is widely regarded as a transitional album for the Beatles. Released in December 1965, it represents the beginning of the second phase of their career - the end of the "mop top" era and the beginning of their more sophisticated, studio-driven sound. They would continue to tour through the summer of the following year, but they had already begun to change.

So, too, did the women who populated their songs.

From *Please Please Me* through *Help!*, those women had barely *been* women; they were scarcely more than girls, from the *her* Paul saw standing there to the *you* whose hand John wants to hold, they are teenagers – objects of young love and desire. The Beatles' early hits are a compendium of valentines to these two-dimensional stand-ins for actual lovers.

With *Rubber Soul*, this changed. With *Rubber Soul*, the girls became women – and formidable women, at that.

This is evident from Track One, Side One - "Drive My Car", in which Paul encounters a woman pursuing a career as an actress, who suggests that he can become her chauffeur – he can "drive her car," which of a course is just code for sex.

The point of the exchange is that it is the woman, and not Paul, who's in charge: she's the boss, the one dangling a job in front of him; viewed euphemistically, she is likewise the sexual aggressor in the scenario. Paul is just responding. This level of female empowerment – in a pop song! - is virtually unprecedented in 1965 England.

Next is John's turn in the hot seat – or it would have been, if the woman in "Norwegian Wood" had any chairs in her flat. This thinly-disguised confession of infidelity on John's part tells of an elicit encounter in the woman's home (see "Norwegian Wood", below) likewise empowers the woman, damn near emasculating John in the process.

From the first line - "I once had a girl, or should I say she once had me" - equal footing is established, with additional ground swiftly surrendered by John as the tale unfolds and the two stay up late drinking – only for John to find himself sexually rejected.

It's a breathtaking, almost inexplicable confession, rending the singer powerless and at the mercy of this strong, self-possessed woman.

Later, Paul encounters a woman who is much the opposite of the aspiring actress; "Michelle" is sophisticated, captivating – and just as elusive. Paul finds himself almost pining, trying to convince her of his passion and resolve.

And John finds himself pining as well, for the "Girl" who seems to utterly own him, tying him in anxious notes as he struggles to process his desire for her in the face of his realization that her domination is slowly unraveling him.

Then there are the biographical tunes – Paul's "You Won't See Me" and "I'm Looking Through You" and George's "If I Needed Someone".

Both of Paul's tunes, written about his relationship with Jane Asher and the frustrations he endured, coping with her independence (see "From Me to You: Dear Jane", page 136), are almost embarrassing confessions to the world that she has the upper hand in the relationship. Paul's writing about the intimate details of their bumpy love life seems to be an attempt to level the playing field, but it falls flat; Jane is one woman of *Rubber Soul* who clearly isn't so easily put in her place.

George's song is more subtle. Written for girlfriend Pattie Boyd, who became his wife the month after *Rubber Soul* was released, "If I Needed Someone" is a man's confession that the woman he's singing to is the one he *really* loves (as opposed, supposedly, to the one he's actually with). The song has a rueful tone, an air of regret; in real life, this regret was avoided, but the song clearly communicates a man conflicted.

It's true that women of substance had surfaced earlier in the Beatles canon – the women of "Day Tripper", "Ticket to Ride" and "Yesterday" were surely not Beatlemaniacs – but as of *Rubber Soul*, we detect a distinct sea change in the Beatles' lyrical narrative, the appearance of a woman that now challenges them as men, forcing them to think about women and relationships in new ways.

"Norwegian Wood"

As Paul became more and more romantic, John grew more and more dysfunctional.

His masterpiece "Norwegian Wood", which leaps off the first side of *Rubber Soul* and blows the listener's mind as it dazzles the ear, is a kind of sequel to "If I Fell" - a thinly-veiled episode of infidelity, written in very transparent code, and more clearly autobiographical than its predecessor.

"I was trying to write about an affair I was having without letting me wife know," John said later, "so it was very gobbledegook. I was sort of writing from my experiences, girls' flats, things like that... I was very careful and paranoid because I didn't want my wife, Cyn, to know that there really was something going on outside the household. I'd always had some kind of affairs going, so I was trying to be sophisticated in writing about an affair, but in such a smokescreen way that you couldn't tell." He finished the song off in St. Moritz, Switzerland in February 1965 – ironically, on holiday with Cynthia.

The song was about an affair, "but I can't remember any specific woman it had to do with," he would later say. His childhood pal and Quarrymen bandmate Pete Shotton identified the woman as a "sophisticated lady journalist" whom his biographer Ray Coleman further labeled "prominent."[26]

Shotton was also able to shed light on some of the song's other lyrical content, recalling the Gambier Terrace flat John had shared with early Beatle Stuart Sutcliffe in Liverpool: "He also managed to allude to his habit, back in his poverty-stricken Art School days, of burning furniture in the fireplace," Shotton reported, adding that in those days, John would sometimes ask guests to "sleep in the bath."

---

[26]There is speculation as to who this "prominent, sophisticated lady journalist" was. Many have thought it to be Maureen Cleave, the writer at the heart of the "Bigger than Jesus" flap; Beatle biographer Philip Norman insists it was Sonny Freeman, wife of photographer Robert Freeman, on the strength of her being Norwegian and having an apartment decorated with wood paneling.

It was Paul who prompted John to include the bit about lighting the fire, though in Paul's mind, John isn't burning furniture in the fireplace – he's burning down the flat, "not that it's any big deal."

The centerpiece of the song is, of course, the affair itself – a true story. It's here that John's dive into imagery not only conveys the many emotional layers of the event, but demonstrates an almost unsettling composure in articulating its adversarial context. It's impossible not to imagine being in the room, and evokes an experience in the listener that could be melancholy, provocative or disturbing, or even all three at once.

"The speaker ponders the nature of a past affair, particularly in terms of the ironic, and, in hindsight, confounding difference between his and his lover's expectations for the liaison," wrote music historian Kenneth Womack. John's narrative makes painfully clear that the woman commands the situation, and he is forced to wrestle with the impact of that reality on his presumptions about their relationship. "The woman's tempestuous laugh offers a clear signal about her obvious control of the situation, and it is highly suggestive, moreover, that she intends to take carnal possession of the speaker on her own fiercely independent and uninhibited terms," Womack continued.

With astonishing economy – there are only 10 lines in the entire song – John proceeds to paint a scene that is both vague and painfully detailed: "I once had a girl, or should I say, she once had me" immediately rips open the wound the song is documenting, turning the tables on the speaker and conveying loss, distress and self-consciousness in a single line. The song continues to say more with less as he continues, "She asked me to stay and she told me to sit anywhere / So I looked around and I noticed there wasn't a chair" - *She invited me into her world, but there was no place for me.*

The ambiguity and the between-the-lines narrative goes on: *"I sat on a rug, biding my time, drinking her wine / We talked until two, and then she said, It's time for bed"*, making clear that the speaker has romantic anticipations – until the woman takes the next step: *"She told me she worked in the morning and started to laugh / I told her I didn't and crawled off to sleep in the bath.*" Is she leading him into sex, or shutting sex down? Next, she laughs, and the speaker goes to sleep in the tub. Because he was spurned, or because he was made too uncomfortable to proceed?

"He's been *had* alright, and by a woman who, without the faintest hint of passion, devises an emotionless, antiromantic one-night stand," interpreted Womack. The utter frustration and disillusionment conveyed in the lyric bespeak the complexities of modern relationships, and John's brilliant imagery paints a word-picture of that complexity, leaving it suitably unfinished on the easel – another perfect choice.

"The song... really ends with a question: 'Isn't it good, Norwegian wood?'," wrote musical analyst John Stevens. "Lennon could not have picked a more ambiguous ending."

The admirable economy of the lyric is echoed by the minimalist melody and musical structure. The song is a sparse verse-refrain, with no chorus or bridge – AB, but with recurring A, and identical melody in both As, a surprise to the listener and a repetition that implies the speaker is going round and round in his own head, reliving the puzzling evening over and over – an elegant Escher loop. The structure also creates an emotional loop, from which there is no escape: by circling back endlessly, rather than ever moving forward, the music underscores the frustration of wanting more and not getting it – exactly what the speaker has experienced.

The song is in E, the "Heaven" key, and the tone and melody of the A section seem welcoming, at first; the waltzish 12/8 time signature is emotionally pleasing. And the length of the A section – only 4 bars, the shortest in all of John's music – puts the listener deceptively at ease.

But there's more going on here. The A section melody is rendered in Mixolydian mode, allowing the melody to proceed from B to lower-octave B, up- and down-stepping with each phrase – it, like the chord structure, never resolves, never returns to E. The up-and-down melodic pattern is also a brilliant reflection of the speaker's mental state, trying to make sense of events as they unfolded – and falling from an emotional high to an emotional low.

The refrain is more revealing still, as the melody shifts to E melodic minor Dorian. The notes run high to low, as in the verse, but no longer bounce up and down: from E, the melody jumps back to B, lingering 4 beats, dropping a step, lingering 4 beats, and so on, under a lyric (in both refrains) that documents the words and actions of the woman – emphatic, decisive... controlling. And at the same time, it ratchets up the tension.

This is musical innovation on a level John had never before achieved – a perfect casting of melody and structure as metaphor, merging notes and lyric into a stark emotional portrait.

While it's easy to be critical of the behavior – cheating on his wife – that inspired the tune in the first place, we can at least credit John with major progress in songcraft – and, in an odd way, a more forthright presentation of himself. "Norwegian Wood" may not present an admirable man, but it certainly presents a candid one.

"The loss in 'Norwegian Wood' comes from the same vulnerability as in 'If I Fell'," wrote Tim Riley, "but this time Lennon knows he's got only himself to blame for the emotional risks he takes."

"If I Needed Someone"

Up steps George, introducing a new style of self-expression that increases the diversity of the Beatles' love song messaging while telling the world quite a lot about himself.

Unlike his previous "Don't Bother Me", a Lennon-esque exercise in self-pity in which a guy who's so miserable without his girl that he feels the need to tell everyone else to go to hell, "If I Needed Someone" has the singer dangling his interest in his woman in a creative way, all while seeming aloof:

If I needed someone to love
You're the one that I'd be thinking of
If I needed someone...

His aloofness is transparent, as he lets slip his true feelings:

Had you come some other day
Then it might not have been like this
But you see now I'm too much in love

He wraps his message up with another tease of faux indifference:

Carve your number on my wall
And maybe you will get a call from me
If I needed someone

In this *Rubber Soul* track, "George's musical personality is still awkwardly earnest, but at the same time his best song yet sounds relaxed and confident," according to Tim Riley. He attributes its success to the riff around which it is built – a riff written in mid-1965 after George had picked up on a similar one in the Byrds' "The Bells of Rhymney". So interesting and vibrant is the riff, achieved by playing a standard D chord in seventh position with a capo (making it a tonal A chord) that George didn't deviate from it: the song is essentially an Indian drone on

A (excepting the bridge), with only a one-step down-shift to a G chord at the end of each second line in the verses[27] (Paul's bass remains on A). The variation in the riff is achieved by the great utility of the standard D finger position, which makes it easy to move smoothly from note to note on the top string.[28]

The song is romantic only in that it is a confession of love, despite its patronizing tone. It possesses none of Paul's warmth, but its transparency is intentional, rather than clumsy, like John's (though the latter was clearly willing to take his messaging much further).

George and Pattie were already married at this point, so it's safe to say the song is more an exercise than a declaration of any kind. Even so, it is a demonstration that George's songwriting voice is growing stronger and more nuanced, with an intensifying awareness of the emotions that are possible in the craft and that the band's experimentation in this domain could benefit from his input.

---

[27] John uses exactly this structure later on "Tomorrow Never Knows", though that song is in the key of C, rather than A.

[28] George would return to this technique and bring it to full maturity in the intro to his final Beatles contribution, "Here Comes the Sun", four years later.

"We Can Work It Out"

As we approach the midpoint of the Beatles' eight-year recording career, we see Paul in the lead when it comes to maturity as a writer of love songs (if not as an actual lover – we have to give that to George or Ringo at this point in the story). And not just maturity; he also shows the most growth, in terms of songcraft and self-expression, since the *Yeah YeahYeah* days.

Well, all good thing must come to an end. While "We Can Work It Out" continues Paul's long streak of steady improvement in songcraft, its messaging leaves a lot to be desired.

This downturn is a consequence of long-term relationship. Paul and Jane had been together for well over two years when he wrote "We Can Work It Out", and the career clash they couldn't move past was a constant challenge. The Beatles were touring themselves to death, and slamming out albums and singles at breakneck pace; Jane, on the other hand, was a rising star of the theater, doing quite a lot of touring herself with her theater company.

The song's wonderful hook – its title phrase, set to anthemic melody that begs the listener to bombastically join in - belies its true content. Paul, seen to be increasingly provincial and old-school man-of-the-house when his attitudes about women are subjected to even mild scrutiny, is indulging very openly in an unfettered expression of masculine (and subtly threatening) self-centeredness:

Try to see it my way
Do I have to keep on talking 'til I can't go on?
While you see it your way
Run the risk of knowing that our love may soon be gone

followed by

Think of what you're saying
You can get it wrong and still you think that it's alright

Think of what I'm saying
We can work it out and get it straight, or say good night

...and with each of these overbearing, selfish proclamations (which boil down to *"I'm right! You're wrong!"*), everything is sunny right away, as Paul invokes that stirring hook that *everyone* just loves:

We can work it out!
We can work it out!

It is John, who contributed the middle eight, who ultimately redeems the song, inserting a decidedly uncharacteristic surge of optimism and reconciliation:

Life is very short, and there's no time
For fussing and fighting, my friend
I have always thought that it's a crime
So I will ask you once again...

George also uplifts the song with his contribution of the waltz-time measures that populate John's middle eight, an almost unnoticed suggestion of dance – another dollop of redemptive optimism.

Recorded on October 20 and 29 of 1965, the song became the group's 13th #1 single.

Love Letters on the Radio

We've noted that each of the three songwriting Beatles wrote songs to the women in their lives – songs that were explicitly biographical, direct communications between lovers. And we've noted that this is not unconventional, in the realm of pop/rock music (or any other genre, for that matter).

What's unusual in this arena is when that communication between lovers winds up all over the radio.

Each of the many real-love-story songs of the Beatles made their way from the songwriter's notebook to the studio to the record shop to the ears of his lover; but in a few cases, there was an extra stop – Top 40 radio.

Here they are.

And I Love Her

If you're Jane Asher and you're Paul McCartney's girlfriend, there really couldn't be a better lead-off song to expose your private business on the airwaves. "And I Love Her", the fifth track from the album *A Hard Day's Night* and its third single to be released (on July 20, 1964), is a haunting, lovely song, a marvelous work both in composition and execution. It expresses a deep and earnest intimacy, rendered in romantic and almost melancholy terms. It is the sentiment of a man who's head-over-heels for his woman, and unafraid to say it in the most vulnerable terms.

At some point, Jane had the experience of turning on a radio and hearing,

> *Bright are the stars that shine*
> *Dark is the sky*
> *I know this love of mine*
> *Will never die*
> *And I Love Her...*

It didn't hurt that the track was one of the richest, most nuanced tracks they had yet produced, with lush, articulate acoustic guitar work, subtle percussion and soaring vocal.

"And I Love Her" was so good, in fact, that it immediately established Paul as the top-shelf balladeer he had always longed to be (see "And I Love Her", page 65) - and he did it a full year before the release of his signature ballad "Yesterday". And it established him, for Jane, as a boyfriend willing to shout his love for her from the rooftops.

We Can Work It Out

Having firmly proclaimed his love for Jane from radios across the known world, Paul then proceeded to start unraveling that accomplishment with the next Paul-and-Jane entry.

"We Can Work It Out", released in December 1965, is beloved by millions for its reconciliatory hook-chorus title and its unrelentingly optimistic middle-eight, which proclaims,

Life is very short, and there's no time
For fussing and fighting, my friend
I have always thought that it's a crime
So I will ask you once again...

All well and good. But the verses themselves, upon review, are far less conciliatory and optimistic:

While you see it your way
Run the risk of knowing that our love will soon be gone

and

While you see it your way
There's a chance that we might fall apart before too long

Fully appraised, the song is an appeal to Jane to relent and give Paul his way, in whatever argument they were having at the time – not exactly the stuff of stalwart romantic partnership. One can wonder what Jane thought when she heard it, along with thousands of others, while driving her car.

Note that it was John, not Paul, who wrote that stirring, upbeat middle-eight.

The Ballad of John and Yoko

John outdoes Paul in sentiment, if not musical and lyrical sophistication, with "The Ballad of John and Yoko" - a one-off single recorded by just the two of them in 1969, destined to be (in one of the most ironic contradictions of the Beatles' career) both the last Beatles UK #1 single and banned by the BBC.

If you're Yoko in 1969, you've already heard yourself immortalized by John on *The White Album* ("Happiness is a Warm Gun"). Now you have an even greater treat in store, when you tune in to the Top 40 station and hear this rocking lament of your unjustly-disparaged relationship, misunderstood by the harsh, unsympathetic establishment. It stokes that you-and-me-against-the-world sentiment that defines your couplehood:

> *Made a lightning trip to Vienna*
> *Eating chocolate cake in a bag*
> *The newspapers said, 'She's gone to his head,*
> *'They look just like two gurus in drag'...*

The song is pure persecution complex laid over a rocking backbeat, tons of fun to the ear, silly and fun on many levels. But it's also an authentic page from the Lennon-Ono diary, capturing perfectly the moment in time immediately following their Gibraltar nuptials. Yoko had to have enjoyed hearing it on the radio, and must have been thrilled when it went to #1 – vindicating the two of them after years of public disdain.

Something

And now George joins the list, at the very last possible moment. "Something", from the swan song album *Abbey Road*, was actually his first A-side single with the Beatles – and his last chance to proclaim his love for wife Pattie on the air.

He'd written several songs for her that had made their way onto Beatles albums (see "From Me to You: Pattie's Greatest Hits", page 196), but none had the power or artistry of this magnificent track, which is nothing short of a masterpiece (See "Something", page 214).

Something in the way she knows
And all I have to do is think of her
Something in the things she shows me
I don't want to leave her now
You know I believe and how...

Pattie is used to adulation – she will, eventually, receive more of it than she knows what to do with (see "For the Love of Pattie", page 181) - but this has to be an experience like no other: "Something" goes to #1 in the US and eventually becomes the second-most covered Beatles song ever, after "Yesterday". Everyone in pop/rock, it seems, all the way up to Frank Sinatra, is singing her song.

Then there were the B-sides.

Why do we care about B-sides? Because they are, by definition, inextricably bound to A-sides, and thus sometimes end up with airplay that album tracks never see.

Thus we have a handful of Beatles love songs which capture real relationship stuff that snagged at least a little bit of airplay.

Don't Let Me Down

Excluded from the album *Let It Be* by producer Phil Spector, "Don't Let Me Down" cried out to be heard by the world. Its placement on the B-side of Paul's "Get Back" was inevitable, given the latter tune's commercial superiority, but it was nonetheless deserving of the world's ear.

If "The Ballad of John and Yoko" had been an anthem of relationship solidarity, this second 45rpm offering from him to her was a paean to that solidarity's underlying intimacy. As Paul did years earlier in "And I Love Her", John establishes unambiguously the sheer depth of his passion for his woman:

I'm in love for the first time
Don't you know it's gonna last
It's a love that lasts forever
It's a love that had no past

And he proceeds to get almost embarrassingly graphic in his praise:

And from the first time that she really done me
Oh she done me,
She done me good
I guess nobody ever really done me
Oh she done me
She done me good

Had to have been a good time for Yoko, when DJs started flipping the disc and sending that one out.

For You Blue

And George is back with this entirely endearing tune for Pattie from *Let It Be*. "For You Blue", a country-ish, blues-based track that landed on the flip side of "The Long and Winding Road" (the Beatles' last #1 single as a band), may not be as masterful as "Something" - but as a love song to wife Pattie, it's even more intimate:

I've loved you from the moment I saw you
You looked at me, that's all you had to do
I feel it now, I hope you feel it, too

and this:

I want you in the morning, girl, I love you
I want you at the moment I feel blue
I'm living every moment, girl, for you

Pattie's hearing some of what Yoko's hearing – utter devotion, stated not just earnestly but with unapologetic vulnerability.

Paul should have been taking notes.

Things We Said Today

The B-side of "A Hard Day's Night" elevated Paul's troubles with Jane in the public arena as "We Can Work It Out" had, but with greater subtlety. The song, tellingly platformed in a minor key, gives plenty of lip service to the sentiment that he and Jane are "deep in love", but can be summed up as a thinly-veiled complaint about the distance between them, as he Beatles around the world and she tours with her acting company, increasingly out of his reach:

Someday, when I'm lonely
Wishing you weren't so far away
Then I will remember
Things we said today

All of that said, the track – which is smart, well-executed, and (as always) utterly listenable – is yet another in a long parade of tracks the Beatles produced between 1965 and 1969 that showcase aspects of relationships that don't normally get attention in pop/rock, let alone on the air.

"In My Life"

If Paul stumbled a little as a human being with "We Can Work It Out", John stepped his humanity up a bit – more than a bit, really - with "In My Life".

He had said that "If I Fell" was a "precursor" to "In My Life", and that could mean several things: both songs are semi-autobiography, and both are attempts for John to get his feelings sorted and expressed. With this latter song, he did a better job of it than he'd ever done before...

...or, by some measures, than he ever would again: "In My Life" might be the greatest love song he ever wrote, in the ears of many. Its sentiment, earnest and clear, is utterly relatable and easy to embrace (as opposed to Paul's in "We Can Work It Out", which is rude and petulant).

He goes wistfully nostalgic in the first two verses (also new for him), but not maudlin; his recall is honest and realistic:

There are places I'll remember
All my life, though some have changed
Some forever, not for better
Some have gone, and some remain

All these places have their moments
With lovers and friends I still can recall
Some are dead and some are living
In my life, I've loved them all

He was worked up the courage to reference his deceased mother Julia (yet another first),[29] and wraps up this section of the song with an expression of appreciation. Now he takes the song higher still, addressing a non-specific "you", emphatically stating that for all the love he's experienced in his life thus far, the *you* he is singing to transcends all of it:

---

[29] The "some are dead" reference also included Stu Sutcliffe, whom John unquestionably loved.

> *But of all these friends and lovers*
> *There is no one compares with you*

and

> *Though I know I'll never lose affection*
> *For people and things that went before*
> *I know I'll often stop and think about them*
> *In my life, I love you more*

The song was, to some degree, a first draft of "Strawberry Fields Forever"; the notion of writing about their childhood, which John and Paul first conceived while planning *Rubber Soul*, inspired an early version of "In My Life" that included references to actual places and events from John's Menlove Avenue youth, later removed.

Kenneth Womack also suggests a more subtle inspiration from John's childhood – a schoolboy reading of Charles Lamb's "The Old Familiar Faces", written more than a century earlier:

> *For some they have died, and some they have left me,*
> *And some are taken from me; all are departed*

Origins aside, John later called it his "first real major piece of work." It's not hard to agree: Womack called it *"Rubber Soul's* most significant and lasting composition."

"In My Life" was recorded on October 18 and 22, 1965 (concurrent with "We Can Work It Out").

"Michelle / Girl"

Our critical perusal has shown that the competition between John and Paul, in the area of love song composition, often had them tackling the same themes at the same time, with revealing results. "If I Fell" and "And I Love Her" found them each struggling to write a love ballad worthy of Perry Como; "Ticket to Ride" and "Yesterday" were their respective competitive efforts in the "She Done Dumped Me" category.

Now, as the band was finding the maturity and experimentalism that would define their sixth album, *Rubber Soul*, as a true artistic departure, they each took their best swing at the "Girl I'm Pining For" genre.

Yet again, John and Paul are writing about exactly the same thing at exactly the same time. In both songs, the singer is expressing passion for a woman who obsesses him. In both songs, this obsession is tinged with the dark realization that something isn't quite right, and the pursuit isn't exactly the healthiest emotional option.

Paul's "Michelle" is by far the more elegant expression, though both songs are musically and lyrically excellent in any case. It's more than just his seductive use of French (tempting us to recall Gomez Addams), or the Parisian sidewalk atmosphere created by the band's superb arrangement; with his usual admirable economy, he underscores his obsession with three revealing verbs:

I love you, I love you, I love you,
That's all I want to say

I need to, I need to, I need to,
I need to make you see

I want you, I want you, I want you,
I think you know by now

And it's not just the glaring *love, need,* and *want*; it's the repetition of each that clarifies the singer's desperation. Everything else we might learn about this woman must be derived from the obsession itself, for Paul offers us *no descriptive assist at all*. He tells us *nothing* about this woman! We infer everything from his over-the-top worship. The only other piece of information conveyed is that Paul intends, despite his obvious failure thus far, to somehow connect with her: *I'll get to you somehow... I'm hoping you will know what I mean... until I find a way.*

Then again, Paul conveys a touch of his message in the music itself, which makes use of the song's parallel minor (the song's verses are in the key of F; the bridge sections shift to Fm), darkening its tone when Paul states an intention.

John's "Girl" also reeks of desperation, but in a far less subtle manner. Jumping right into his sad tale without intro or even supporting instrumentation, he sings not to the girl but to everyone else:

Is there anybody going to listen to my story
All about the girl who came to stay?
She's the kind of girl you want so much, it makes you sorry
Still you don't regret a single day

From that point on, he paints a damning portrait of a lover who is cold, manipulative, insincere and even insulting, taking advantage of him, seemingly draining away his very life. Yet he can't tear himself away from her, though he's tried again and again.

Here's where things get odd, intriguing, but a little disturbing: when John was later asked who inspired the song, he replied that the lyric is about his "ideal" woman: "I always had this dream of this particular woman coming into my life... I know it wouldn't be someone buying Beatles records. I was hoping for a woman who could give me what I get from a man intellectually. I wanted someone I could be myself with."

The gaudy, awkward sexism of patriarchal Liverpool aside, it's breathtaking to consider that John's "ideal" could be a woman who would abuse and humiliate him so. And yet, in the chorus, we hear him just singing her generic name: *Girl*... postscripted with a lascivious intake of breath that underscores his brainless, ill-advised lust.

Like Paul, John skillfully juxtaposes major and minor keys. When just singing about the girl, in the refrain, he's in the major key of E♭; when he switches into storytelling mode, trying to comfort himself and draw attention to himself, he goes to the relative Cm.

"Michelle" was recorded November 3, 1965; "Girl" was recorded the following week, on November 11.[30]

---

[30]The anxieties and insecurity that are so clear in John in "Girl" find resolution and are expunged when we hear "Woman" 15 years later, in the final month of his life.

"You Won't See Me"

Just when Jane Asher was experiencing "We Can Work It Out" all over the radio, fully aware that the world would wonder whether Paul was ranting about her, this track presents itself on *Rubber Soul*.

If Paul was patronizing in the earlier song, he was positively condescending in this one. He is *literally complaining openly about Jane's busy schedule*, setting their actual argument to music:

When I call you up
Your line's engaged

And as if that isn't bad enough, he then insults her with

I have had enough
So act your age

This pity party goes on and on:

We have lost the time
That was so hard to find
And I will lose my mind
If you won't see me

He then stoops to melodrama:

Though the days are few
They're filled with tears
And since I lost you
It feels like years

Yes, it seems so long
Girl, since you've been gone
And I just can't go on
If you won't see me

Once again, Paul uses some musical sleight of hand to get away with a lyric that should be far beneath him: the melody and backing track are bright and upbeat, belying the song's petulant message. The music is so outrageously cheery, in contrast to Paul's rant, that John and George resort to a jaw-dropping, ludicrous *"oo-la-la-la!"* chant behind the verses.

All of that said, the music's delicious Motown groove, along with Paul's spirited bass line, make it an exemplary track, worthy of many repeats. If we didn't know exactly what he was really saying and who he was really saying it to, he'd have gotten away with something here. And we don't much care.

The track was recorded November 11, 1965 – damningly, the same day as John's "Girl".

"The Word"

And now, mercifully, John and Paul serve up an actual collaboration for *Rubber Soul* - "The Word", a generic love song that celebrates the spirit of love without getting into all of the mess and bother.

It was a marijuana-fueled collaboration in which the two were anticipating the upcoming Summer of Love; they even did a psychedelic lyric sheet in crayon (the song explicitly foreshadows John's soon-to-be-conceived mega-anthem "All You Need is Love", which of course defined the latter Sixties). "The Word" was more John than Paul, but both injected plenty of words and music into the mix.

"The Word" marks the transition between the boy-meets-girl love of Beatlemania and the peace-and-harmony love of the hippy era," wrote Steve Turner in *A Hard Day's Write*. "The love that John was now singing about offered 'freedom' and 'light'. It even offered 'the way'. He may even have been thinking of 'the word' in the evangelistic sense of 'preaching the word'."

The lyrics do, indeed, almost come across as slogans embedded in a sermon:

Say the word and you'll be free
Say the word and be like me

and

Spread the word I'm thinking of
Have you heard the word is love?

Now that I know what I feel must be right
I'm here to show everybody the light

"Sermon" is no stretch. Billy Graham could have uttered these words in a football stadium. These lyrics would feel at home in *Godspell*.

The universality of the song was a Beatles first, but they would continue writing similar songs for the rest of their days together. "They were in tune with the times, and the hippie community quickly recognized them as soul mates," wrote Jean-Michel Guesdon and Philippe Margotin. No kidding!

John's take: "[Love] seems like the underlying theme to the universe. Everything that was worthwhile got down to this love, love, love thing. And it is the struggle to love, to be loved, and express that (just something about love) that's fantastic.

"Even though, I'm not always a loving person, I want to be that," he went on, without bursting into flame. "I want to be as loving as possible."

The song was recorded November 10, 1965, ironically the night before "Girl" and "You Won't See Me" - two songs that weren't even remotely loving.

The Beatles Guide to Love & Sex

1966:

And When I Awoke, I Was Alone

"For No One"

Paul had done quite a lot of whining about Jane on *Rubber Soul*, and the months between that album and *Revolver* – an even stronger evolutionary step for the band – he'd clearly done a lot of brooding.

"For No One" is a break-up song, no question, but it's a particularly pensive one; the singer is obsessing over his lover's change in mood and attitude, moving on emotionally before he has. It's not hard to read Paul and Jane into that scenario; she was clearly very much her own person, without the cloying need to devote herself Paul that he seemed to expect.

The song is an unacknowledged masterpiece, on a par with "Yesterday" and "Eleanor Rigby" among Paul's priceless gems, but hasn't gotten the recognition the others have. Even so, critics and musicologists have steadily praised the song from the moment it popped out of *Revolver*'s second side, huddling inconspicuously between the fluffy "And Your Bird Can Sing" and the quirky "Doctor Robert".

Journalist Maureen Cleave,[31] for instance, wrote that the song was "as moving as 'Yesterday'." Critic Thomas Ward called the song "one of the most inspired of the singer's whole career... a simply beautiful song, full of idiosyncratic McCartney touches yet undeniably inspired." John himself called it "one of my favorites of his; a nice piece of work."

The lyrics, written from a detached but pensive point of view, describe a love gone cold:

And in her eyes, you see nothing
No sign of love behind the tears
Cried for no one
A love that should have lasted years

There's some self-pity going on here, because the singer's ego has taken quite a body slam; but there's a poignance not only in

---

[31] Remember her? She's the leading suspect in "Norwegian Wood".

the singer's circular sorrow and puzzlement, as he can't let go until he fully understands what went wrong, but in the music beneath, where warmth and gentleness and forward motion persist, even so.

It's hard to overstate just how beautiful that music is. It's almost all Paul, playing piano, bass and clavichord (Ringo added percussion), and its construction is masterful. The verses are in B major; the melody is simple, a kind of conversational arpeggio; the underlying chords flow downward in a gentle progression, as the singer offers his in-the-moment observations. Then comes the chorus, which shifts abruptly to a harsh, almost jarring C#m, the supertonic minor; the melody anxiously rises, becoming more frenetic; the singer is starting to lose it a little as he describes the deadness in his lover's eyes.

And at the end of each chorus sits a suspended dominant, waiting there, unresolved - and the song cycles back into a verse. The song is saying, through the structure of the music, that the singer hasn't figured anything out yet – he's going in circles. And, brilliantly, the song *ends* that way, hovering, unresolved – just as Paul was at the time, in his situation with Jane.

The gorgeous French horn on the track is the work of Alan Civil, "the best horn player in London," per engineer Geoff Emerick - recruited by producer George Martin to provide not only the classy baroque vibe the song called for, but some emotional counterpoint. The solo, which Civil concocted improvisationally, has nothing at all to do with the rest of the song; it's a musical metaphor for the woman Paul is singing about, just going her own merry way - "immaculate indifference," in Ian Macdonald's words. Yet there's a wistfulness in Civil's playing, intended or not, that weds the emotion of the solo to the quandary of the singer. Civil then resurfaces in the final verse, inserting instrumental counterpoint behind the singer's line – two melodies talking past each other.

Simple as it was, the song took three sessions to complete, between May 9 and 19 of 1966. It remains one of Paul's greatest works, however unacknowledged – and a somber page in the documentation of his relationship with Jane.[32]

"Here, There, and Everywhere"

Elsewhere on *Revolver*, Paul served up a love song that is believably generic: he credited his inspiration to rival Brian Wilson of the Beach Boys, who had recently stuck a burr in Paul's saddle with the glorious masterwork *Pet Sounds*. Specifically, Paul was nudged by the track "God Only Knows", the chords of which "Here, There, and Everywhere" mimic early on.[33]

From there, Paul's lyrics reflect his sunny romantic idealism:

Everywhere
Knowing that love is to share
Each one believing that love never dies
Watching her eyes, and hoping I'm always there

He wrote the song while sitting by John's pool, waiting for him to wake up on a sunny morning. Kenneth Womack's interpretation, then, isn't surprising, stating that the song is about "living in the here and now."

Adding to the veracity of the song's generic nature is Paul's artful construction of the verses around the words in the title: he built the first verse around the word *Here*, the second around *There*, the third around *Everywhere*. The song truly was an exercise in songcraft, a challenge Paul set himself to as he waited for John to drag himself out of bed.

Both Beatles would later rank "Here, There, and Everywhere" as one of the Beatles' best. Per Steven Turner, it is "widely regarded as his greatest love song."

It was one of the last tracks completed for *Revolver*, recorded on June 14, 1966.

---

[32] In his retrospective comments about "For No One", Paul waffled about its origins. He initially claimed the song was written about his first experience living with a woman after first leaving home as a young man, but later confessed it was about another argument he'd had with Jane. It's due to this sort of equivocation that we never quite take him at his word in such matters.

[33] Ian Macdonald disputes this recollection, pointing out that Pet Sounds wasn't released in England until a month after Paul had written the song.

Yoko Ono

It was at the Indica Gallery in London, owned by the Beatles' friend John Dunbar, that John met Yoko Ono for the first time.

The day was November 7, 1966, and she was preparing a conceptual exhibit of interactive art at the gallery. John sauntered in, and Dunbar introduced them. John perused Yoko's art, starting with a ladder painted white that led to a magnifying glass. Looking through the glass, John found the word YES written on the ceiling in very tiny letters, and was instantly charmed.

(At that meeting, she claimed to be unaware of who the Beatles were, but that's disingenuous; not long before that opening, she had met Paul at his home, asking for an original manuscript of Beatles lyrics to contribute to a John Cage project.)

"The first impression I had of him was that he looked very beautiful, a very elegant kind of guy," Yoko later recalled. "There was a nice feeling about it."

Thus began perhaps the oddest of Beatle romances – the dark, tormented Beatles genius who had no idea how to love or be loved, and the tiny, shapeless Japanese artist who never seemed to smile.

Yoko began to write to John, and they corresponded through much of 1967, until John sponsored another exhibit of Yoko's work in September.

The more they communicated, the more their minds began to intertwine. "It's not like he simply understood what I was trying to do," Yoko said. "We were on the same wavelength."

The exchange of letters now included phone calls, and Yoko thought nothing of calling him at the home he shared with Cynthia, who demanded to know who she was. John dismissed the calls as a "bullshit" avant-garde artist's pleas for money.

Finally, the spring of 1968, Yoko was in London to perform with Ornette Coleman. Cynthia was on holiday in Greece, so John invited her over to his Kenwood house. He took her to his home studio and they spent the night making tape loops, and finished the night by having sex.

With uncanny timing, Cynthia returned home, finding Yoko in her robe and the two of them drinking tea.

"When Cynthia came in on us, I immediately tried to sit a little bit further away from John," Yoko said. "John said, 'No. Don't worry about it. It's okay.' He grabbed my hand and we were sitting together. He wanted it that way. I don't know why."

Cynthia then did the strangest thing imaginable. She had entered the house with two friends, and when John first saw her, he said, simply, "Oh, hi."

She responded with the first thing she could think of: "We were all looking forward to dinner in London after lunch in Rome and breakfast in Greece. Would you like to come?"

"No thanks," he replied.

"The stupidity of that question has haunted me ever since," she would later write.

Many histories emphasize that in Yoko, John had found his true love, and had then set his sights firmly on their future together. According to Cynthia, however, he reverted back to his usual dissembling.

"We talked of our failings and faults, our love for each other, our hopes and dreams. John talked again about his other women, and insisted that Yoko was no more important than they had been. 'It's you I love, Cyn,' he said. 'I love you now more than I ever have before.'" He took her to bed, just to underscore the point.

It didn't take. Whatever he'd said to Cynthia, he continued his headlong rush into his relationship with Yoko. She became a constant presence in his life, attending *White Album* and then *Get Back* sessions, even singing back-up vocals here and there.

The public got wind of John's new relationship on June 19, the morning after John and Yoko had attended a show at the Old Vic theater with the other Beatles, dressed in matching white outfits. The press went wild, and Yoko was heckled. The next day, "Every front page in Britain trumpeted the month-old fact that John Lennon had left his wife and begun an affair with Yoko Ono," reported Philip Norman.

In that flurry of months in 1968, Yoko would become the fourth woman impregnated by a Beatle out of wedlock, and she and John recorded the baby's fetal heartbeat, which made it onto their avantgarde album Life with the Lions. Yoko then miscarried.

On March 20, 1969, John became the first Beatle to marry for a second time, in a ceremony on the Isle of Gibraltar in Spain. He would soon immortalize the occasion in a #1 Beatles single.

Determined to push back against a skeptical press and a very critical fan community, Yoko said, "When people get cynical about love, they should look at us and see that it is possible."

The tortured Beatle had finally found love. He had yet, however, to find happiness.

"Love You To"

The newly wed George had been emboldened both by his songwriting successes on *Rubber Soul* and his romantic successes with Pattie, whom he'd married in January of 1966. He had also become notable in rock circles in general for his successful deployment of Indian music, with his sitar lines in "Norwegian Wood" and the near-drone foundation of "If I Needed Someone". Now he stepped it up with "Love You To", a song that was overtly Indian in tone and structure.

A love song written for his new wife Pattie, "Love You To" is also "part philosophical," according to Ian Macdonald. Both the love and the philosophy present unapologetically:

Each day just goes so fast
I turn around, it's passed
You don't get time to hang a sign on me

A lifetime is so short
A new one can't be bought
But what you've got means such a lot to me

I'll make love to you
If you want me to

With "Love You To", George followed his bandmates' lead in departing from the boy-girl Beatleisms of the past. His lyrics here are somewhat dreamy – that is to say, LSD-fueled – but also balance humor with a touch of dread and distance. Robert Rodriguez wrote that the song is "a somewhat oblique expression of love directed toward his bride, along with larger concerns regarding mortality and purpose." Ian Inglis found integration in the lyrics, writing that they "remind us that in a world of material dissatisfaction and moral disharmony, there is always the solace of sexual pleasure."

Wilfred Mellers found more integration still:

"Love You To" is "A Beatle incantation or love-spell. In this song there is, of course, no harmony, in the Western sense, only a tonic and dominant tone over which sitar and voice embroider melismatically. The vocal line oscillates around G, moving up to B♭, the flattened seventh, down to F natural; and the music convinces not because it is 'like' genuine Indian music (it is by Indian standards rudimentary), but because it is an extension of the anti-Western, anti-materialism, anti-action theme we have seen to be endemic in Beatle music. Though George seems to be singing (as did all the early Beatle songs) of sexual love and presumably of coitus itself, his point is that the act of love can destroy the temporal sense ('make love all day, make love singing songs'): which is what happens in the drone-coda and fade-out."

Adding to the dreamy atmosphere of the song were authentic Indian tambura to provide the drone, tabla for percussion, and sitar for texture – courtesy of George's friends in the Asian Music Circle.

His newfound boldness went beyond "Love You To"; he wrote three tracks on *Revolver*, a first for him.[34]

The track was recorded early in the *Revolver* sessions, on April 11 and 13, 1966.

---

[34] The other two tracks are "Taxman" and "I Want to Tell You."

"She Said She Said"

This, the first literal acid trip to make it onto a Beatles album, has already been celebrated above for its exceptional pronouning; but its real value is in the discomfited self-portraiture it achieves with its stark depiction of John's inner dilemma.

"She Said She Said" may be the most bareass-naked we ever see him in a Beatles song, his insecurity and angst paraded with the awkwardness of a drunk wearing a lampshade. That he had few if any boundaries as a lyricist is well known, but this song represented a new threshold in unfiltered self-expression.

The song was born in August 1965, "after an acid trip in LA during a break in the Beatles' tour where we were having fun with the Byrds and lots of girls," John told *Playboy* in 1980. "Peter Fonda came in when we were on acid and he kept coming up to me and sitting next to me and whispering, 'I know what it's like to be dead.' He was describing an acid trip he's been on."

Fonda remembered it differently; he wasn't telling George about an acid trip, he was referring to a clinical death experience he'd had as a child.

"I remember sitting out on the deck of the house with George, who was telling me that he thought he was saying," Fonda later said. "I told him that there was nothing to be afraid of and that all he needed to do was to relax. I said that I knew what it was like to be dead because when I was 10 years old I'd accidentally shot myself in the stomach and my heart stopped beating three times while I was on the operating table because I'd lost so much blood. John was passing by at the time and hear me saying 'I know what it's like to be dead.' He looked at me and said, 'You're making me feel like I've never been born. Who put all that shit in your head?'" In a burst of acid-fueled belligerence, John had Fonda expelled from the party.[35]

---

[35]Fonda had other recollections of the evening: "I had the privilege of listening to the four of them sing, play around and scheme about what they would compose and achieve. They were so enthusiastic, so full of fun. John was the wittiest and most astute. I enjoyed just hearing him speak and there were no pretensions in his

There's much to work with here.

First, we note that the lyric is practically a transcript of the conversation John had with Fonda:

She said
"I know what it's like to be dead
I know what it is to be sad"
And she's making me feel like
I've never been born

So literal is this transcription that John had originally planned to call the song "He Said He Said", and included the lines

I said
"Who put all that crap in your head?
I know what it's like to be mad
And it's making me feel like my trousers are torn

The gender flip is revealing in a number of ways, but mostly in that it serves to underscore the significance of the middle eight, which reads

When I was a boy
Everything was right
Everything was right

Kenneth Womack makes much of this, quoting an analysis by Jacqueline Warwick: "Note that Lennon counters the woman's creepy tale by invoking the homosocial universe of his boyhood days at school, when 'everything was right.' The song presents heterosexual relationships negatively, depicting a woman who will not stop talking and a man who doesn't want to listen (but has difficulty tearing himself away)."

"Part of the song's complexity is its primal urge: the wish for innocence," wrote Tim Riley. "A woman glibly tells the singer she

---

manner. He just sat around, laying out lines of poetry and thinking – an amazing mind. He talked a lot yet he still seemed so private."

knows what it's like to be dead; the singer shoots back that she's making him feel like he's never been born. His thoughts become scattered, and the confrontation sets off nagging worries and renewed aggravation; the exchange is trivial, but what it summons up is overwhelming – her smugness makes him feel impossibly small and defenseless. The intensity is palpable; the singer is wrestling with feelings he barely understands – inadequacy, helplessness, and a profound fear. Because Lennon so obviously feels these emotions as he plays and sings them, the music is a direct connection to his psyche."

The music, which is predictably brilliant, reflects John's own psychic stammering; the rhythm is irregular, the opening guitar jarring and harsh.

Underscoring the utter transparency of John's narrative, in contrast to Paul's papering-over of his own emotions with idealistic sentiments, is the fact that the latter didn't play on the track, which was laid down on June 26, 1966. He had stormed out of the studio after an argument.

"The trouble [with Paul] is that he wants the fans' adulation and mine, too. He's so selfish. That's his biggest fault. He can't see that my feelings for him are real and that the fans' are fantasy."

~Jane Asher

The Beatles Guide to Love & Sex

1967:

You're Gonna Lose That Girl

Beatlesogyny

As positive and love-affirming as the Beatles are known to be, they have their dark side.

It's been made clear above a number of times that the Fab Four weren't as evolved as men as their adoring fans may have imagined them to be. They were boys trying to become men, and that's a transition fraught with disillusion and peril, no matter who you are. Their immaturity, their lack of understanding of women, and their lack of self-awareness in this delicate domain all manage to surface from time to time in their songs.

Getting Better

This *Pepper* tune by Paul, otherwise a gem both musically and lyrically, includes a second verse - *"I used to be cruel to my woman, I beat her / And kept her apart from the things that she loved"* - that defies explanation. How is it conceivable that *any* Beatle thought this line was a good idea? And is it possible George Martin let it pass without comment?

You Can't Do That

It's John's turn to be the asshole, writing here about laying down the law to his girl, when it comes to other guys: *"I've got something to say that might cause you pain / If I catch you talking to that boy again"*. Wut? Really? Sounds like a threat. Because it is.

"Please listen to me if you wanna stay mine/I can't help my feelings, I go outta my mind/I'm gonna let you down, and leave you flat/cause I told you before/you can't do that."

John *is* an asshole, when it comes to possessiveness and jealousy, and so toxic was this lyric that the song, originally intended for inclusion in the film *A Hard Day's Night*, was cut. Thank Zeus.

I'll Get You

There's some ambiguity here, it must be said; this more-or-less innocent-sounding tune, which sits on the flip side of the "She Loves You" single, says *"Imagine I'm in love with you"* - and that's a message female fans were just fine with.

But the song proceeds to condescend into domination, stating pretty plainly that the woman has no agency here: she isn't being given a choice, where the relationship is concerned: *"You might as well resign yourself to me,"* she is told, don't even think about leaving., because *"I'll get you in the end"*.

Sounds a bit ominous...

I'll Follow the Sun

Here Paul introduces *ghosting*. That sort of behavior sits high in our shared consciousness today, but back then, not so much; Paul actually wrote this song when he was 15, and clearly never gave a second thought to the fact that he was describing a deeply selfish and disrespectful attitude:

One day you'll look
To see I've gone
For tomorrow may rain
So I'll follow the sun

Yup, I'm outta here, I left without warning or explanation. Heinous enough when it happens today online, but in the Sixties – pre-Internet – it literally meant the spontaneous abandonment of a flesh-and-blood relationship.

That's bad enough, but he adds a touch of cold condescension:

Some day you'll know
I was the one
But tomorrow may rain

So I'll follow the sun

From bad to worse: *he's* the one doing the ghosting, but let's makesure she realizes that *she's* the one who's losing something special.

Probably the most disturbing thing about this attitude is Paul's apparent complete lack of self-awareness. The message of this song is basically, *I'm an asshole, and I really don't care what you think of that.* Not the sentiment of a loving guy.

Run For Your Life

As bad as the line in "Getting Better" is, the content of "Run for Your Life" is worse, representing an all-time low in Beatle lyrics.

The opening line of the song - *"I'd rather see you dead, little girl, than to be with another man"* – sets the tone for a song that goes beyond disturbing; it's flat-out *alarming*.

Defenders of the song, who claim that John is singing the part of some invented character, have a hard time justifying the lines that follow: *"Catch you with another man / that's the end, little girl"*... *"Let this be a sermon / I mean everything I've said / Baby I'm determined / And I'd rather see you dead"*.

The singer is bluntly informing his lover that if he learns she's been unfaithful, he will murder her. It's hard to imagine a more toxic, misogynist message.

To be sure, John squares up his theme in the second verse: *"Well, you know that I'm a wicked guy / And I was born with a jealous mind"*. Got it; yes, we know John himself was prone to jealousy and perhaps it's to his credit, to some degree, that he expunged this emotion by being open about it (his song "Jealous Guy" says it all). But can't we have a song about jealousy that doesn't go as far as homicide?

This is, of course, the really ugly stuff. But misogyny comes in many shapes and sizes, and we've already noted (repeatedly) that those subtler shadings can, unfortunately, be found in other

Beatles work. Paul's all-too-public condescension toward Jane Asher, evident in "We Can Work It Out", "You Won't See Me", "What You're Doing" and other songs, stand out; this is the patriarchal I-Expect-My-Woman-To-Serve-Me male mindset at its most disappointing.

These complaints of misogyny among the Fabs are by no means quibbles; they are serious markers of immaturity, selfishness – and in John's case, perhaps even outright pathology – but they are by no means the entire story. Watch for "You Say You Want a (Sexual) Revolution" below...

"Lucy in the Sky with Diamonds"

LSD may have given John the schizophrenic frenzy of "She Said She Said" - but it didn't give him "Lucy".

The idea that **L**ucy in the **S**ky with **D**iamonds is code for **LSD**; has been long since debunked; we know for certain that the title derived from kindergarten art generated by his son Julian.[36] And while it is easy, all the same, to ascribe the fantasia of the "Lucy" lyrics to John's brain's acid bath, the wild imagery is more feasibly accounted for by the inspiration of Lewis Caroll.

But "Lucy" is far more than just wild imagery; it is a complete departure for John, where writing about women is concerned.

Over the five years thus expired in the recording career of the band, John has pinballed between autobiographical confessions of infidelity, toxic masculinity, and consequential self-loathing; now he gives us a phantasmagorical profile of his ideal woman – and she scares the shit out of him.

The song describes a journey as well as an interaction with a woman, and its three verses each provide a phase of that journey:

> *Picture yourself in a boat on a river*
> *With tangerine trees and marmalade skies*
> *Somebody calls you, you answer quite slowly*
> *A girl with kaleidoscope eyes*

The next step is to

> *Follow her down to a bridge by a fountain,* where
> *Everyone smiles as you drift past the flowers*

And finally, *on a train in a station,*

> *Suddenly someone is there at the turnstile,*
> *The girl with kaleidoscope eyes*

---

[36]The Lucy in the song was Julian's classmate Lucy O'Donnell, an actual person.

In "Strawberry Fields Forever", written and recorded only a couple of months earlier, John had resorted by surreal images as a retreat from anxiety. It's no stretch to view "Lucy" as an extension of that same reflex, this time incorporating a fantasy woman. His Lucyscape is a place of sun and flowers and great beauty, complemented by the accommodations of smiling automatons; the "girl with kaleidoscope eyes" is a siren, summoning him into that world, leading him through it, and then – train and turnstile – is she staying behind as he departs? Is she wanting him to stay? Is she about to follow him somewhere else?

The "journey" aspect of the song is, lyrically, its strongest feature. John serves up several forms of locomotion – a boat on a river, newspaper taxis, and the train in the station, with strolls in between. Where was John before? Where he is going now?

What the hell is going on here?

"There was also the image of the female who would someday come save me - a 'girl with kaleidoscope eyes' who would come out of the sky," he said. "It turned out to be Yoko, though I hadn't met Yoko yet... The imagery was Alice in the boat. And also the image of this female who would come and save me - this secret love that was going to come one day. So it turned out to be Yoko, though, and I hadn't met Yoko then. But she was my imaginary girl that we all have."

John is misremembering or misreporting here, in this conversation that occurred in a 1980 interview. He *had* met Yoko by that time – on November 9, 1966. Even so, the idea that "Lucy" is actually Yoko might be too simple: John's "imaginary girl" may not be just one girl, but a morphing succession of women. Per Ian Macdonald,

"The 'girl with kaleidoscope eyes'... was, for Lennon, the lover/mother of his most helpless fantasies: 'the image of the female who would someday come save me'," wrote Macdonald. "This mysterious, oracular woman—mourned for in 'Yes It Is', bewildered by in 'She Said, She Said' - was originally his mother, Julia, a role subsequently assumed by Yoko Ono."

Once we consider "imaginary girl" Lucy as John's savior, a mother-amalgam of Julia and Yoko, we can then scrutinize exactly what he's saying in the song.

To this end, we can turn to Tim Kasser's *Lucy in the Mind of Lennon: An Empirical Analysis of Lucy in the Sky with Diamonds*, in which the author invokes linguistic analysis to determine John's state of mind in the song. This mission initially pursues the question of whether the lyrics were written while John was actually high, but the analysis turns up an even more intriguing result:

"The lyrics of 'Lucy in the Sky with Diamonds' are actually more similar to how people write and speak when they are lying and when they are attempting to psychologically distance themselves from painful psychological material," Kasser writes. "Rather than expressing the bevy of emotions that typically occur when one is tripping, and that Lennon often expressed in other songs, 'Lucy in the Sky with Diamonds' is almost barren of feeling."

John almost slipped one past us there, it seems; "Lucy" doesn't *seem* barren of feeling, because we feel rushes of emotion in response to the dazzling images he offers us – and the mystery of his fantasy woman likewise stirs our feelings, as many of us have such fantasy lovers tucked in our memories.

John's lyrics, while offering us an in-the-moment description of a personal experience, are *not* offered as a first-person chronicle, but as a detached, guided meditation: *Picture yourself*, the singer instructs the listener; *Follow her*, he suggests. We're being invited into his dream, but he's disengaged from that dream; we're being sent in as proxies.

"Rather than focusing on the experience of the here and now, the lyrics of the song avoid the self and the present, and instead focus on the abstract, the intellectual, and that which is outside of one's self," Kasser continues. "Emotions, of course, are notoriously 'here and now,' and rarely abstract.

"In sum, these analyses suggest that while Lennon was writing these lyrics, he may have been rather wary of engaging the present moment, his own inner experience, and his emotions."

Recorded March 1 and 2 of 1967, "Lucy" became the "gateway" song into the freaky, fun milieu of *Sgt. Pepper's Lonely Hearts Club Band.*

From Me to You: Dear Jane

All three of the songwriting Beatles wrote songs to their women. Cynthia may have only gotten a couple of lines, but Yoko got several songs, as did Pattie.

Paul, however, was far and away the champion, when it came to communicating to Jane on vinyl. He wrote so many songs to or about her that it's even possible to set up categories: 1) songs that were overtly to Jane; 2) songs that might have been to Jane; 3) songs that may not have been to or about Jane, but which echo what was going on in their relationship, all the same.

Since the point of this exercise is to try to suss out what the songs tell us about the men who wrote them, we'll just go ahead and look at all of them.

The earliest love song to Jane really started out as a poem, as we saw above; "All My Loving", which appeared on the sophomore disc *With the Beatles* is a terrific first effort in the writing-about-my-girl genre, but it's interesting because it introduces right away the component of their new relationship (they'd only met about six months before the album came out) that would not only define it, but would become the primary impetus for all the Jane songs to follow: their frequent separations and the pressure their respective careers would put on that relationship.

Points for Paul on the next song, one of his very best and one of the finest love songs the Beatles would ever release - "And I Love Her", on *A Hard Day's Night*, which followed eight months later. This one also gets points for not being a song sung to Jane, but a song where Paul is singing about Jane – he's telling the world about his love (*"And if you saw my love, you'd love her, too"*).

Ah, but then the first glimmer of trouble appears. On the same album, "Things We Said Today" appears. This, too, is a song about separated. While the lyrics wax on about precious moments, the song is tellingly in a minor key, with an almost somber melody line. Soon, Paul's Jane songs will be somber in more ways than one.

On *Beatles for Sale*, which arrived at the end of 1964, Paul serves up two more Jane songs. "Every Little Thing" is a fine tune, another song where Paul is telling the world about his lady. It's full of promising endearments, but it also lets slip a hint of his provincial attitude that it's a woman's job to be subservient. The other song is less subtle: "What You're Doing" is the first openly whiny song about how Paul doesn't like it much that Jane is unavailable. Which, as her acting career soared, was increasingly the case.

"Another Girl", appearing the following summer on the *Help!* soundtrack, may or may not have been written with Jane in mind. It's Paul's version of "Norwegian Wood", a song about a man in a relationship with one woman while he's focused on another woman. The difference here is telling: John was singing to the listener, not the woman – telling the world a story about her. Paul is singing to his woman about this other woman. It's a not-very-veiled threat: *And so I'm telling you this time you'd better stop / For I have another girl.*

History has already revealed that there were many, many other girls, so it's hard to know exactly whether this song is about any particular one; it's perfectly possible that the song is abstract, and in no way autobiographical. We may never know.

Whether or not the sea change in the Beatles' songwriting (see "The Women of *Rubber Soul*", page 86) was being the next two songs or whether Paul was simply growing bolder and more reckless is hard to tell. But his two Jane songs on that album were so blatant that they must have embarrassed her or angered her (or both): a Jane song on a Beatles album was now beginning to feel like having to listen to a couple arguing in the middle of a dinner party, oblivious to all the other guests.

"You Won't See Me" can be viewed as a response to Jane joining the cast of a Bristol Old Vic theater production as the album was being made. They fought so heatedly over this that they briefly broke up. For a while, Jane wouldn't take Paul's phone calls (*"When I call you up, your line's engaged"*). Bad enough that Paul wrote about this in a Beatles song, but he then proceeded to refer to her with insulting condescension (*"I have* had enough, so act your age"*). Miraculously, they reconciled, and lived to fight another day.

"I'm Looking Through You" is more of the same (*"Why, tell me why did you not treat me right"*), this time with more not-so-veiled threat (*"Love has a nasty habit of disappearing overnight"*). Paul described the song as "cathartic" in retrospect, but it's hard to grasp how he can reconcile the sentiments he's expressing with the man the world believes him to be.

The buyers of the record, of course, didn't have our benefit of hindsight. For all they know, Paul was writing about no one in particular, inspired by something he saw on television. Those who hadn't read in the newspaper that he and Jane were a couple might even assume that he had a girlfriend who truly was as vain and selfish as the girl in his song.

"We Can Work It Out" then appeared as a single (see "We Can Work It Out", above), setting a new record for self-centeredness in a Paul song. And yet, its buoyant chorus and John's encouraging middle-eight can distract the listener completely from the song's blatant narcissism.

Finally, *Revolver* – the last Beatles album where Paul sings about Jane.

Neither of these last two Jane songs is sung *to* Jane – they are both *about* her. And they are polar opposites.

"Here, There and Everywhere" is, mercifully, a worthy expression of love and endurance, without the whining and threats. There's a smidge of the provincialism - "I need my love to be here", "If she's beside me," and so on – but it's balanced with some reciprocation.

And finally, "For No One" (see above) - a song that is essentially an epitaph for their relationship. Appearing in August 1966, almost two years before Paul and Jane would break up for good, the song documents the growing deadness in their relationship and ruefully notes the ways they've changed. The chorus - "And in her eyes, you see nothing / No sign of love behind the tears / Cried for no one / A love that should have lasted years" - is so cold and bitter, it could have been in a Fleetwood Mac song.

There are almost enough songs here for an album. You could easily spin up a Paul and Jane playlist or mix CD. Such an album would have its bright moments, of course; but, taken as a whole, what would it be saying to the listener?

"When I'm Sixty-Four" / "Lovely Rita"

Paul's first "letter" song, "P.S. I Love You", had been followed up by "Paperback Writer" ("Dear sir or madam, will you read my book?"). Now comes yet another, and it's probably the most letter-like of them all.

That letter is written by a young man to an old woman, imagining what their life together will feel like on the far side:

When I get older, losing my hair
Many years from now
Will you still be sending me a valentine,
Birthday greetings, bottle of wine?

It's a sweet sentiment, too corny to be maudlin, and rendered as it is with George Martin's bouncy clarinets and the band's musical eye-rolls Easter-egging deep in the mix, it's irresistibly likable.

It's also perfectly placed on Side Two of *Pepper*, snapping the listener out of the cosmic trance of "Within You Without You" and setting up the all-too-worldly "Lovely Rita" to follow. The song is written as an endearment, and it serves exactly that function on the album – inviting the previous generation to join in the current generation's fun.

That previous generation included, of course, Paul's father Jim McCartney, himself a musician and coincidentally (or not) a man of 64 at the time the song was recorded. Its music-hall vibe was crafted specifically with Jim in mind; Paul had, in fact, written the song a full decade earlier, when he was still a young teenager.

That being the case, we can see the song as a snapshot of the very young Paul's idealization of love and marriage: two aging folks still doting on one another, exasperating one another and celebrating one another, decades into their lives. It's innocently idealistic, irresistibly charming:

I could be handy, mending a fuse
When your lights have gone
You can knit a sweater by the fireside,
Sunday mornings, go for a ride

Doing the garden, digging the weeds
Who could ask for more?
Will you still need me, will you still feed me,
When I'm sixty-four?

As for the "letter" part, there's the singer's entreaty that his hoped-for wife will

Send me a postcard, drop me a line
Stating point of view

And signs off with

Yours sincerely, wasting away

The format is perfectly chosen: the singer doesn't just mention valentines; the song itself practically *is* one.

Paul clearly is looking for something very different from what John is after. His concept of domestic bliss may have some provincial overtones in the gender-roles department, but he's not looking for either a savior or a servant; he's looking for an actual partner. For this reason, "When I'm Sixty-Four" may have been the most promising love song yet, at the time it was recorded.

Not everyone sees it that way, of course. "Paul takes the Beatles' study of consciousness into the existential uncertainty of the sunset years," wrote Kenneth Womack. "The song is written as a letter from a socially inept young man who seems to be trying to coax a female he hardly knows into promising him long-term devotion," wrote Steven Turner, offering the cynical interpretation that "The official tone of the letter... paints a convincing picture of this formal young gent who wants to get it all in writing before he signs on the dotted line."

That's a fair reading, but George Martin went on to verify that the song is no parody; Paul had all the respect in the world for the music of his father's generation. And he certainly viewed his parents' marriage as something to aspire to.

Moreover, time would prove Paul's sincerity; as we see below, the love he describes in "When I'm Sixty-Four" is exactly the love he eventually went for, with Linda.

Jarringly, Paul's idealized wife-of-many-years is immediately juxtaposed with a *wham-bam* off the street (literally) in Rita the Meter Maid, casting aside as inconvenient the warm, domestic values he has just espoused with a gesture. Interesting that as John is painting his fantasy woman as ethereal, Paul is profiling his as not only workaday but an authority figure to be conquered.

The implied subtext is that Paul, having been ticketed by Rita, is trying to get out of the ticket by seducing her (on the couch, as her younger siblings look on). The implications there are too goofy to really take seriously, but are certainly in keeping with the *Pepper* pastiche. It's also a colorful entry in Paul's growing catalog of off-beat paperback-writer narratives about "ordinary" people.

Then again, the shallowness of "Rita" may be biting Paul in the ass; just as the *tit-tit-tit-tit* bridge backing in "Girl" spoke to the Beatle's persistent schoolboy immaturity, the orgiastic panting in the coda of "Rita" is hard to view as anything other than an early version of the childish, misogynist preening that will saturate MTV in the upcoming Eighties.

"When I'm Sixty-Four" was the first track recorded for the album, on December 6 and 20, 1966; "Rita" was recorded later, on February 23-24 and March 7 and 21.

Beatlesex: Naughty Bits

Before they ever entered the studio, the barely-20 Beatles had already spent hundreds of hours in British and German clubs, playing for attractive, willing young women. Even George, only 17 on his first road trip, gained plenty of erotic experience as an up-and-coming Beatle.

All of that road sex translated into an already-world-wise sensibility as the Beatles began to write and record their own songs. Even "Please Please Me," the title track of the first album, was really about reciprocal oral sex.

From there, the sexual references in Beatle songs committed to legend are a mixture of interview confessions, analysis by critics and fan speculation. Some are overt ("Why Don't We Do It in the Road?"); some are implied ("fish and finger pie," in "Penny Lane"); some are just guesses ("...meeting a man from the motor trade," thought to be a reference to prostitution, in "She's Leaving Home").

"Drive My Car" Paul's first true excursion into veiled sexual content was a clever (and, for him, surprising) role reversal: "Baby" in the song is the man, and the woman is offering sexual favors in exchange for help with her career – a story Paul would later act out for real with Francie Schwartz (see page 165).

"Girl" The backing vocals on the middle eight are *"tit-tit-tit-tit-tit-tit-tit-tit."* At the time, a suspicious George Martin asked what they were saying, and they innocently answered, *"dit-dit-dit-dit!"* Paul has long since confessed that wasn't true.

"Day Tripper" *"She's a big teaser"* was originally *"She's a prick teaser,"* but they couldn't get away with it.

"Back in the USSR" Paul's metaphorical masterpiece rivals John's "Happiness is a Warm Gun" in inventiveness: *"Oh, show me round your snow-peaked mountains way down south / Take me to your daddy's farm / Let me hear your balalaikas ringing out /*

Come and keep your comrade warm", with its references to breasts and orgasms, is certainly the more playful of the two.

"I Saw Her Standing There" In all fairness, Paul's original opening line was originally *"She was just seventeen, never a beauty queen,"* but the change to *"She was just 17, you know what I mean"* inserted a wink-wink into a lyric that implied a felony, coming out of the mouth of a 24-year-old.

"Penny Lane" *"A four of fish and finger pies"* is Liverpool slang for fingering a young woman's genitals.

"With a Little Help from My Friends" In a moment of best-friend cruelty, John and Paul gave Ringo the line, *"What do you see when you turn out the light / I can't tell you but I know it's mine"* to imply that he was sleeping alone and jerking off.

"Ticket to Ride" *"The girl that's driving me mad is going away / She's got a ticket to ride, and she don't care".* On the surface, it's a generic break-up song, and the girl is just climbing on a train and leaving. In fact, "ticket to ride" refers to something the Beatles learned about prostitutes in Germany: they received medical cards testifying that they were STD-free. The meaning of the song, then, is that John's girlfriend is leaving him to become a hooker.

Ouch...

"I've Got a Feeling" The last song that John and Paul wrote together was a combination of Paul's "I've Got a Feeling" and an unrealized John song called "Everybody Had a Hard Year". In the end of the song, they slipped in, *"Everybody had a wet dream."*

"A Day in the Life" The orchestral build-up was explicitly imagined and implemented as a 'musical orgasm.'

"All You Need is Love"

"All You Need is Love" is, on its face, certainly a love song; but it's less a song *expressing* love as it is a song that *explains* love – or, at least, love as John had come to conceive it in the summer of 1967.

He must have been onto something – because, of course, the summer of 1967 is now and forever regarded as the Summer of Love, and "All You Need is Love" was its anthem.

We've already noted above that "The Word" was the song's precursor, invoking the same laser-focus on the universality of the heart's deepest song. In this culmination, John couldn't be more clear: the word love occurs no less than 66 times in the lyric.

Beatles manager Brian Epstein seized on this clarity in unveiling "All You Need is Love" as the text of the band's role in *Our World*, the first true global telecast, in which they represented Britain on June 25, 1967. "It was an inspired song and they really wanted to give the world a message," he said. "The nice thing about it is that it cannot be misinterpreted. It is a clear message saying that love is everything."

Then again, part of that clarity derived from John's television addiction, and his fondness for slogans; the song's chorus is exactly that:

All you need is love
All you need is love
All you need is love, love
Love is all you need

The absolutist language of the slogan pervades the song, leaving no wiggle room for argument or doubt: *All* you need is love; *Nothing* you can do that can't be done; *nothing* you can sing that can't be sung; *no one* you can save that can't be saved. This concession to the that-settles-it nature of love is very un-John-like, from a certain point of view, as he at times had been very much at home in ambiguity. Here, however, he's setting a tone, and he sets it with great effectiveness.

What is John-like about the lyric is John's "internal contradictions (positivisms expressed with negatives) and bloated self-confidence ("it's easy")," wrote Tim Riley, "[making] it the naïve answer to 'A Day in the Life'."

His cohort in this is George Martin, who assembled a score that was downright bombastic, bursting with color and noise and a touch of the absurd; Paul was likewise an accomplice, embedding touches of self-effacing, self-mocking self-reference in the background.[37]

Paul also came alongside Brian in touting the song's utopian ideals, which did indeed lay out the blueprint for the hippy community that was standing in the wings, primed to embrace the band:

"We had been told that we'd be seen recording it by the whole world at the same time," he said, "so we had one message for the world – love. We need more love in the world."

Kenneth Womack's take is a little more substantive:

"Rather fittingly, 'All You Need is Love' witness the Beatles bidding farewell, in a manner of speaking, to their early years, as well as to the naïve, idealistic visions of love that brought them world fame in the first place," he wrote. "[It] eschews the egocentric bliss of romantic love to extol the anticupidity of *caritas* – a divine and spiritually-minded love for all humanity."

Released as a single two weeks after the *Our World* broadcast, on July 7, it became the band's 18th #1 single.

---

[37] Supporting tracks for the broadcast were pre-recorded, leaving nothing to chance, on June 14, 19, 23 and 24, 1967.

Oedipus Rocks

There has been a great deal of speculation among critics, fans, and pop music pundits as to how much of the Beatles' output displays actual Oedipal impulses and emotion.

If one looks at the music, there's much to discuss. Many have analyzed the lyrics of both John and Paul, and come up with a great many references to Julia and Mary, their respective mums.

In the case of Paul, there has been speculation that "And I Love Her", "Lady Madonna", "Let It Be" and "Yesterday" all contain references to Mary. Paul has acknowledged one of these specifically:

When I find myself in times of trouble,
Mother Mary comes to me
Speaking words of wisdom
Let it be

"Mother Mary" is the departed Mary McCartney, and Paul is not shy about letting us know that. On the other hand, there's nothing remotely sexual about the reference: he misses his mother's presence and counsel, and would give anything to see her once again. That's how most of us would feel.

There is speculation that *I said something wrong, now I long for yesterday* is Paul's covert confession and penance for his callous reception of the news that Mary had died. If true - there, too, no real Oedipal conflict. "And I Love Her" is an explicitly sexual song, so a case could be made there – if anything in the song even remotely qualified as a reference to Mary McCartney. Ditto "Lady Madonna", which profiles a woman who was nothing whatsoever like Mary – except that she was both sensual and a saint.

Nor was there anything in Paul's personal history that hinted at an Oedipal conflict in his mind.

John, of course, is another story.

"Julia" openly parades his mother as goddess, and John's worship is romantic to the core. He doesn't even remotely speak in code, and is so overt in his choice of words that is it clear he is crediting the feelings he is transferring to Yoko, his new lover, to his deceased mother (see "Julia", page 191).

He would go on to write even more such expressions in his solo work, including "Mother" and "My Mummy's Dead", in his struggle to resolve his complicated feelings. ("Woman", the last such song, was created in the final months of his life, by which times we can suppose his feelings about Julia had been resolved; or, at the least, he had transferred all of his romantic energy to Yoko.)

Scrutiny of John's life supports this assumption of mother-love, which surfaced when he was a teenager:

"As his hormones began to run riot, he also became increasingly conscious of Jula's physical allure," wrote Philip Norman, "the more so as she had always treated him in a jokey, flirtatious manner, more like a sportive young aunt."

John himself confessed this in the Lennon Audio Diaries, personal recordings he made that were reported by *Rolling Stone* in 1979:

"I was just remembering the time I had my hand on my mother's tit in Number 1 Blomfield Road, in... off Mather Avenue, near Garston. It's when I was about 14. I took the day off school, I was always doing that and hanging out in her house... and I was thinking, I wonder if I should doing anything else, you know. And it was a strange moment, because I actually had the hots, as they say, for some rather lower-class female that lived on the opposite side of the road. But I always think whether I should have done it, presuming she would have allowed it."

John's biographers have made much of this bombshell, given that it's so breathtakingly candid, but there are many others less overt.

He openly spoke of his feelings for his mother to Yoko, it later came out, in the early days of their relationship. So stark were the recollections he shared with her that it must have become obvious early on to both that the dynamic clarified in "Julia" was what he was seeking in theirs.

"More than anything else, he talked of Julia," Norman wrote, "how beautiful, fascinating, and funny she was, how she had stayed close to him throughout his boyhood yet never properly been 'his,' and what a horrendous gap had been torn in his eighteen-year-old life when a car knocked her down just yards from Mimi's front gate."

John reported just as clearly to Maureen Cleave:

"He told me that when he was in his teens, he sometimes used to be in Julia's room with her when she had a rest in the afternoon," she wrote. "And he'd always regretted he'd never been able to have sex with her."

What does it matter? Well, for a start, it explains how a young man who could devote so many notes and chords and words to the explication of love had so much difficulty expressing it himself; throughout his life, until he met Yoko, no woman could ever measure up to Julia. And it's clear that at the moment in his life when his mother was taken from him, he had grown very dependent upon her in his emotional development – she was his confidante, his encouragement, in ways his mates and girlfriends could never be.

Whatever Paul's deepest inner feelings for his mother, his overt expression of them took the form of reverence and purity – Mother Mary. The world needed to hear of her in "Let It Be", and through that song she lives on in the hearts of millions.

As for John, his life and mother-love and agonizing catharsis may be relatable to some, but the larger lesson of his tortured journey is that love changes over time. Whether or not that change is, in the long run, healthy or empty or creepy is not a random outcome.

"Lady Madonna"

In Elvis's voice, Paul then offered up one the most interesting Beatle commentaries on female sexuality.

Paul's Lady Madonna is the next in a growing line of interesting characters in his pseudo-literary canon, someone to observe, scrutinize and comment upon. Her story is simple (the entire lyric is a mere 19 lines); Paul's commentary is not.

Lady Madonna, children at your feed
Wonder how you manage to make ends meet

Friday night arrives without a suitcase
Sunday morning creeping like a nun
Monday's child has learned to tie his bootlace
See how they run

and

Lady Madonna, baby at your breast
Wonders how you manage to feed the rest?

followed by

Lady Madonna, lying on the bed
Listen to the music playing in your head

With his usual natty yet evocative economy, Paul has conceived a portrait of a complicated woman – and yet she is, in his mind, an everywoman. He's not summoning his dead mother or chasing an angel, as John is wont to do; he's commenting on the burdens society lays on women in general.

"A growling sax exonerates guilty pleasures backed by the vocals' sarcastic "up-bah-bah-bah"s," Tim Riley commented. "With kids running about in the verses and the farcical nursery-rhyme bridge, prolonged innocence is hooted at as unnatural;

sex is congenital. Like the corrupt choirboys in "Doctor Robert", the religious concept of purity is uncovered as a charade."

It's the hypocrisy-of-religion part that constitutes the B-side of Paul's argument here. Kenneth Womack commented:

"McCartney employs the days of the week as the song's structure, pointedly excluding Saturday – there is no Sabbath, no day of rest for Lady Madonna, whose children grow up in spite of her," he wrote. "'See how they run,' the narrator laments, while the unwed mother sells her soul – not to mention her body – in order to make ends meet by any means necessary. 'Lady Madonna, lying on the bed, listen to the music playing in your head.' As she plies her loveless trade, the music washes across her being, transporting Lady Madonna to another world beyond the stale bedroom, beyond her hopelessly expanding ménage. With its explicitly holy antecedent, Lady Madonna's name paradoxically elevates the status of McCartney's heroine, while calling the church's capacity for engendering charity into question at the same time. As with 'Eleanor Rigby', 'Lady Madonna' portrays a world in which, time and time again, an insensate society turns a blind eye to the suffering. No one is saved."

In a 1986 interview in *Musician* magazine, Paul retconned the song as a tribute to mothers everywhere – but that's revisionism at its most brazen. If your hope is to venerate mothers everywhere, you don't do it with Elvis Presley's ironic leer. The entire point of this exercise is to lay bare the truths of society's constraint of sexuality overall – not just the having-babies part.

Recorded February 3 and 6 of 1968, "Lady Madonna" went straight to single, hitting #1 in the UK.

Linda Eastman

It's hard to conceive of a woman more different from the other Beatle wives than Linda. For that matter, it's hard to conceive of a woman more different from Paul's other women than Linda. Perhaps it shouldn't be surprising that she's the one he ended up with.

She was, in the first place, neither from Liverpool nor even British; she was born into an American family of East Coast lawyers, with a borderline upper-class upbringing. She was a free spirit, at ease in her own skin. She was career-minded, but not in the way that Jane had been. She was divorced, and already had a child. On top of all that, she was Jewish.

A photographer, she found a niche for herself that was not unlike the one Astrid Kirchherr had occupied: shooting rock stars. Setting aside her father's hopes that she might seek more formal training and loftier ambitions, she made her way into rock circles, hanging out at Fillmore East and catching Hendrix, Dylan, the Who, the Doors, Simon & Garfunkel, Aretha Franklin, Janis Joplin and others with her camera. She was the first female photographer to have a picture on the cover of *Rolling Stone* – a shot of Eric Clapton on the May 11, 1968 cover.

It wasn't just professional opportunity that drove her into rock music circles; she herself was a huge fan, and of the Beatles in particular. Though she'd had an early crush on John, she had set her sights on Paul long before they actually met.

"She always insisted that she was going to marry Paul McCartney," said Nat Weiss, "even before she met him."

She'd gone to London in May 1967, seeking just that kind of rock community and opportunity when she found herself at the Bag O'Nails Club, where Paul happened to be.

"I was quite shameless, really," she said of that meeting. "I was with somebody else… and I saw Paul at the other side of the room. He looked so beautiful that I made up my mind I would have to pick him up."

Seeing the laid-back, tall woman with the long blonde hair, Paul had a similar reaction. "I spotted her across the crowded club, and although I would normally have been nervous chatting her up, I realized I had to," he recalled.

They saw each other again four days later at the *Sgt. Pepper* photo shoot. A year would pass before they would see each other again.

It was at a press conference in May 1968, where Paul spied her among the photographers gathered for the event. He left with her phone number.

A month later in Los Angeles, where Paul was meeting with Capital Records executives to discuss Apple record distribution, Paul called the number Linda had given him. She wasn't there, so he had to leave a message, letting her know he was in country and the address of the poolside bungalow he was using at the Beverly Hills Hotel.

That bungalow was stocked with willing females by Apple employee Tony Bramwell, and on the second day of the trip, Paul found Linda among them. Immediately, all the others vanished from his mind: she had his full attention.

"As I looked across the room, I suddenly saw something happen," Bramwell later wrote. "Right before my eyes, they fell in love. It was like the thunderbolt the Sicilians speak of, the *coup de foudre* the French speak of in hushed tones, that once-in-a-lifetime feeling."

Perhaps. Paul was still engaged to Jane at the time, and had two other women in the shadows (see "Side Gigs", page 163). But in that moment, he instructed Bramwell to keep his off hours clear of any other women for the duration of their Los Angeles trip.

The summer of 1968 was one of turmoil for Paul. *The White Album* was in progress; "Hey Jude" was blasting out of radios all around the world; and he was breaking up with Jane. It is unsurprising that in the midst of it all, he would reach back out to the carefree woman who had breezed in and out of his life, long blonde hair flowing, promising nothing but her comfortable presence.

On the one hand, Linda was career-minded, just as Jane had been; she took her photography seriously and had been tireless in cultivating the connections that enabled her to make rapid progress in a highly competitive profession. On the other hand, that profession not only didn't take her in other directions; it made Paul the ideal companion. If she wanted to thrive as a photographer in the world of rock music, there was no better place to be than right next to Paul McCartney. And Paul, it was now firmly established, wanted to be with someone who wanted to be right next to him.

Paul was more than smitten; he was bowled over. Linda was unlike any woman he'd ever known.

A couple of things really struck me about her: I liked her as a woman, she was good-looking with a good figure and so physically I was attracted to her, but her mental attitude was, and still is, quite rebellious because she was brought up in this rather lofty, well-to-do world. It wasn't huge conspicuous wealth, but relative to me it was huge wealth. She was the kind of kid who would hang out in the kitchen with the black maids, learning to cook, and she didn't like all the socialising, 'Hello, how are you, I'm the younger daughter of the family.' She used to keep out of the way of all that, so to this day she doesn't like big, rich, empty houses. There was a lot of that where she came from. She was more likely to go on to the empty plot behind the big rich house when the big rich people didn't know she was there in the woods and up-end rocks looking for salamanders. This was one of the big things we had in common because I used to do a lot of that when I was a kid, we both shared a love of nature. That became one of our big links."

In early September, Linda got on a plane and returned to London. And – literally overnight – Paul McCartney became someone new.

It happened when he took Linda to his farm in Scotland, which was as unglamorous as it possibly could be. It was the very definition of rustic, devoid of amenities – but was "the most beautiful land you have ever seen," she said, "way at the end of nowhere."

It would help that Linda was already a mom, and a devoted one; Paul got on easily with children, and Heather was no exception. When she joined her mother in London, Paul would read to her and sing her to sleep.

Just like that, the furtive, unfaithful, deceitful Paul became both monogamous and committed. He'd found his perfect mate. It was a foregone conclusion that he and Linda would marry – which they did, less than six months later, on March 12, 1969.

They would remain married – very happily so – for the next 29 years.

"Hey, man, I have to tell you, I'm in love with your wife."

~Eric Clapton, to George

1968:

You Have Found Her, Now Go and Get Her

Breaking Up is Hard to Do: John and Cynthia

The moment when Cynthia had discovered Yoko in her home, in her robe, with her husband, had been surreal. What happened next was all too conventional.

Oddly, John – the transgressor, however one might look at it – struck the first blow in ending what had been a misbegotten marriage from the beginning. He filed for divorce, citing Cynthia's "adultery".

The hypocrisy of such a gesture could be matched only by its audaciousness. It may have been to do with the fact that Cynthia was, at long last, seeking out the company of another man. That man was an Italian named Roberto Bassanini, with whom she went on holiday in Pesaro in the spring of 1968.

It was Magic Alex Mardas, the quirky would-be genius John had hired to create technical wonders for Apple, who delivered the news to Cynthia: "I'm come with a message from John. He is going to divorce you, take Julian away from you and send you back to Hoylake."

Returning home, she met with John (and, of course, Yoko) at the Kenwood house, accompanied by her mother, who had never thought much of John. "All hell broke loose," according to an observer outside.

And so began their divorce negotiations. Worse than these, however, was the treatment she received beyond John and Yoko: Cynthia, who had been the longest-serving woman in the Beatles family, first Beatles girlfriend, wife, and mother, was "amputated from his life 'like a gangrenous limb'," according to Philip Norman. George and Ringo steered clear of her; even Pattie and Maureen, to whom she'd been a big sister for years, kept their distance.

Only Paul continued to treat her with kindness and respect (see page 160).

And almost on cue, Yoko became pregnant. That quickly, John's cried of "adultery!" vanished, and Cynthia countersued him for the same thing. She was granted a divorce decree nisi, and declined to sue him for half of his assets, though she certainly could have; instead, she accepted an up-front payment of £100,000, with another £100,000 put in trust for Julian. It was official on November 8, 1968.

From Cynthia's standpoint – and, at this point, she'd known him more than a decade – John had become someone different since Yoko had arrived:

"I knew the man up until our divorce," she would later write. "After that, I didn't know the man at all. I worried about the complete change I saw in him. He lost his sense of humor and he got aggressive. He wasn't for the world anymore. He was just for Yoko. Before that, he opened his arms and embraced with world with his wit and his humor. After he met Yoko he was a completely different kind of person."

She bought a house with the money. She then began figuring out how she would live, and what she would do, as the ex-wife of a Beatle.

She would later marry Bassanini, but that marriage would likewise fail.

"Hey Jude"

It's easy to consider "Hey Jude", perhaps the greatest rock anthem ever, as too big to be on a mere list of love songs. Both the lyric and its simple melody are transcendent, speaking to anyone and everyone, the ultimate expression of hope and encouragement.

But it certainly is a love song, and on a number of levels – several of which have been meaning when we consider them in the context of the relationships within the Beatles family.

The surface sentiment, encouragement, is an **I->You->Her** song, in the pronoun-y framework we looked at far above. Paul is singing *to* a friend *about* a girl, offering a kind and hopeful word:

Hey Jude
Don't make it bad
Take a sad song and make it better
Remember to let her into your heart
Then you can start to make it better

The song seems to continue to be more of the same:

Hey Jude
Don't be afraid
You were made to go out and get her
The minute you let her under your skin
Then you begin to make it better

If that's all the song offered, it would still be a marvelous song, worthy of permanent residence in our minds and hearts. But Paul takes it all up a notch:

And any time you feel the pain
Hey Jude, refrain
Don't carry the world upon your shoulders

For well you know that it's a fool
Who plays it cool
By making his world a little colder

This is more than just brotherly advice. Now Paul is expanding his encouragement beyond moving forward into love, urging Jude to a new state of mind where self-love and openness have a place. It's no longer just love advice; it's life advice.

Jude, of course, is Julian Lennon – John's neglected son, now a child of divorced parents, and all of five years old. It is now well-known that Paul, who cared for the boy like an uncle, got in his car and went to visit Julian and Cynthia, offering them warmth and support – and he wrote this song for Julian in the car as he drove.

Both Julian and Cynthia have publicly expressed just how much Paul's visit meant to them,[38] and of course the message of "Hey Jude" is all the more endearing when we know who Paul had in mind when he wrote it – and why he felt it important to share those particular thoughts.

But, of course, it isn't that simple. When John heard "Hey Jude", he assumed it was written for him:

Hey Jude
Don't let me down
You have found her, now go and get her...

John took this as Paul's gentle way of giving his blessing to John's new relationship with Yoko – which, in many ways, replaced their own relationship. Paul would never again be John's confidante, and both knew it; the song was, in John's mind, Paul's acknowledgment of that.

"I always heard it as a song to me," he said. "I took it very personally."

---

[38] "I was touched by his obvious concern for our welfare," Cynthia said in an interview. "I will never forget Paul's gesture of care and concern in coming to see us."

There's also a reading in which Paul is addressing himself – a bit of self-care, given the new presence of Linda in his life and the weight of the band's imminent dissolution beginning to gather above him.

"Paul's vocal performance on 'Hey Jude' gestures toward the sublime," wrote Kenneth Womack. "Rich and buoyant, his voice has rarely sounded better... Lyrically, the song begins with a much-needed bout of commiseration and reassurance from its author - "don't make it bad," "don't be afraid," "don't carry the world upon your shoulders" - and slowly transforms into a tender caution about the ways in which loneliness begets even more loneliness...

"Ultimately, 'Hey Jude' ponders the notion – idealistic, perhaps, during that jaded summer of 1968 – that individual healing is rendered possible through a renewed relationship with the human community that exists beyond the self.

"The composition's lyrics are made manifest by its music, which slowly builds from a solitary voice and explodes, finally, with the joyful sounds of Jude rejoining the wider world from whence he had lost his way."

"Hey Jude" has a message that transcends the band – *take heart, go for it, the best is yet to come!* - and works for Julian, for lovers-to-be, for the world at large. Recorded on July 31 and August 1 of 1968, right in the middle of the *White Album* sessions, it spent a record-breaking nine weeks at #1 and remains, to this day, the core anthem of Paul's live shows.

Side Gigs

Paul had bought a three-story house on Cavendish Avenue in St. John's Wood in 1965, for its proximity to Abbey Road. In 1966, Jane moved in with him. Setting up house, however, did little to bring the two of them closer together; Paul had another US tour coming up, and Jane had joined the Bristol Old Vic theater company, which took her away from home for weeks at a time.

And the physical distance, problematic as it was, really wasn't the problem.

"Jane was no Stepford wife," wrote Philip Norman. "There could be tensions when her independent-mindedness and plain-spokenness ran up against the reality of who her boyfriend really was. Modest and unaffected though Paul might seem, he was an enormous star, courted by the whole world and with a manager and support team dedicated to gratifying his every whim."

This included, of course, women and sex. Having enjoyed an endless supply of indulgent gratification on the road with the band, he was no slow to cultivate accommodation in his own backyard to be accessed during Jane's absences, as the Beatles' touring days ended in 1966.

"Paul always needed to be with a woman," according to author Chris Salewicz. "When he was with one, the tension lines on his forehead and around those liquid, slow-moving eyes would vanish; that cherub's face, so much harder in real life than in photographs, would visibly soften."

Paul had additional motivation: "He hadn't wanted her to join the Bristol Old Vic theatre company and her decision to put this major career step above his wishes created a distance more than merely geographical," Philip Norman wrote. "In Bristol for long periods during play-runs, Jane had been seeing someone else and word got back to Paul. Thus the world's most adored young man had to deal with his first-ever dose of rejection."

"Jane had always had to live with the knowledge that half the young, and not so young, women in the world wanted to sleep with Paul," wrote Norman, "and that for him accepting the sexual opportunities which endlessly came his way counted as only a step beyond signing an autograph. What she didn't know, and never would, was that for almost the whole time they'd lived together at Cavendish he was having a parallel affair with an actress and model named Maggie McGivern."

Paul met Maggie when he visited the home of John Dunbar (the one who owned the gallery where John met Yoko) and his wife Marianne Faithfull, who employed her as nanny to their infant son Nicholas. Waiting for John, and with Marianne out of the house, Paul sat at their kitchen table talking with 20-year-old Maggie.

He began showing up more often, including an evening when John and Marianne were in Paris. He stayed the night, though it was chaste. It didn't stay that way long.

Paul kept Maggie far, far away from any press, but was open about their relationship around the other Beatles and Brian Epstein. She fit in more comfortably with them, as she was a big fan of pot (Jane eschewed drugs altogether).

She even spent the night at the Cavendish house from time to time when Jane was away, cooking Paul breakfast in the morning.

Paul was careful to keep their time together private. "We once went out for a drive in the country in his Aston Martin," Maggie was quoted by Philip Norman. "Ike and Tina Turner's 'River Deep, Mountain High' was blasting out of the speakers, and it gave him the idea for 'Good Day Sunshine'. He started beating out the rhythm on the dashboard.

"He was like a sponge. Whatever was going on around him, he'd soak up and turn into a song."

One would think an accommodation this close and convenient would have kept Paul happy. But he pushed the envelope further still, in the late spring of 1968.

After the death of Brian Epstein in 1967, the Beatles had brazenly (and foolishly) decided to manage themselves – establishing Apple, which was basically a huge tax kite, a place to hide their growing millions from George's Taxman, "investing" in whatever cockamamie artistic schemes struck their fancy. They opened a boutique, started a film company, set up their own record label (the only remnant of the venture, it still exists today), and even an electronics company. They broadly advertised that starving artists could find refuge at Apple, which would generously fund the dreams that the philistine powers-that-be across the creative industries were endlessly turning away.

And across the pond, in New York, a 23-year-old woman named Francie Schwartz decided she would take them up their offer. She had written a treatment for a screenplay, it seemed, and she resolved to present it to Apple. Fired from her copywriting job, she collected her severance pay and flew to London.

Presenting herself at Apple headquarters on Wigmore Street with uncanny timing, she ran right into Paul near the receptionist's desk. She paused to take in the moment.

"Is this it?" she asked herself. "Is this the guy that millions and millions of chicks are moaning and groaning over? Writing letters about and masturbating about, and dreaming about?"

She caught Paul's eye, and he sauntered over to her. She handed him the screenplay treatment, a photo of herself, and her contact information.

The next day, a note arrived at the flat where she was staying with a new friend she'd made her first night in London.

COME, CALL, DO SOMETHING CONSTRUCTIVE read the note.

She called. In the course of the call, it became clear to her that he wasn't particularly interested in her movie treatment; he was focused on her as a young, attractive female.

Paul immediately presented his default condition, that provincial masculine attitude he'd displayed endlessly and even still harbored in his relationship with Jane: he wanted Francie to be at his beck and call, 24/7.

And so began yet another affair, running alongside the one with Maggie, under the cloud of his engagement to Jane.

Paul then vanished for a month that included a Scotland vacation with Jane. Francie waited patiently, and was well-rewarded for her forbearance: when Paul returned, he invited her to Abbey Road, where she sat in awe as the Beatles recorded John's "Revolution". She even got to sing backing vocals.

Several similar evenings left her determined to make her way into Paul's inner sanctum. She sent him a note:

DEAR MR. PLUMP, I THINK I'M GOING TO HAVE TO GO HOME SOON. WHEN AM I GOING TO SEE YOU?

He responded with a telegram: MAKE IT MONDAY, MR. P

He appeared at the flat where she was staying, "brown from sunning himself up in Wales at his brother's wedding," she wrote in her memoir. They had sex.

"...he fell asleep after, and I lay there looking at his face, not sure how to make it seem more real.

"He hadn't been terribly good or terribly bad. He seemed to rush into it, as if thinking about it too much would mean he wouldn't make it."

Paul continued to drop in that way for a quick shag, avoiding any questions Francie might ask about the nature of their relationship. But didn't press it, and her discretion paid off: he eventually brought her to Cavendish Avenue, escorting her through the gate and past the Apple Scruffs who routinely congregated outside.

Inside, he lit a fire in the fireplace and fixed them a drink, then proceeding to wax eloquent on his doubts about his engagement and Jane's commitment.

Francie was no dummy. She'd seen enough in her weeks around Paul to know exactly how to respond.

"If I were your lady, nothing would be more important to me than your happiness," she replied.

"Do you think you could take care of me?" he asked.

"I don't know... we are so different," she answered. "I'd be glad to try."

"Jane is obviously confused as to her priorities and is too selfishly caught up in her own career and doesn't see the obvious need to give it all up for me," Paul said to Francie, according to biographer Chet Flippo. "True love should mean total devotion."[39]

---

[39]Flippo's biography of Paul provides no source or substantiation for this quote. It might be paraphrased, or not even authentic.

And so she moved into the Cavendish house, bringing Paul hot tea in bed each morning.

"It's not important sometimes if a person isn't particularly good in bed," she wrote. "He had his hang-ups, and I think he felt sometimes that he wasn't manly enough. His body was sweet, and beautiful, with almost undetectable curves in it. Nothing to get hung up about, and one could be happy, if one didn't demand too much, or even want too much. The relationship had begun on his 'save me' lament, not on a rush of sexual flashes. But he seemed to have many minds, that untangling the hang-ups in each one would take all the energy in me."

The domestic bliss was shattered when Jane arrived home early (much as Cynthia had done months earlier) from tour, letting herself in and heading up the stairs. Outside, one of the Apple Scruffs tried to warn Paul via intercom, but he didn't hear.

Despite the fact that she lived there, Jane paused at the bedroom door and politely knocked. Paul, in a moment of unfathomable density, actually said, "Who is it?", then tried to slip out of the bedroom in a bathrobe. Jane bolted from the house.

Margaret Asher then showed up, "oozing hostility," on two evenings while Paul was in the studio working on the *White Album*. She methodically packed up Jane's things and took them away. *Trouble in paradise*, Francie realized with a surge of hope.

John would appear at Cavendish Avenue, going on and on about Yoko, which Francie could see bothered Paul. At times John brought Yoko along, and they'd play tapes from the latest session.

"He wasn't happy. But the big things that were driving him mad were beyond me," Francie wrote.

"It might have been merely young and awkward, but our feelings were too uneven to enjoy even then. He was petulant, outrageous, a little Medici prince, powdered and laid on a satin pillow at a very early age. People would come up and pat his ass, as it were. You had to admire him for putting up with it, and understand the difficulty of straying from this spot to take a woman."

John and Yoko were having troubles of their own around this time. John was still married to Cynthia, and their relationship was still a secret. They needed refuge, which Paul provided; the two moved into the Cavendish Avenue house.

Francie got on extremely well with Yoko. "As the two of us cooked breakfast for our respective men, she'd rap with a kind of new, feminine wisdom about how hard it was to make them happy... she was also opening up her wealth of strength and determination to John. All the same, she confided in me that she didn't believe any relationship could last more than seven years."

This didn't last; Paul, his insecurities mounting and the emotional pressure of his collapsing engagement increasing, impulsively sent a note to John: YOU AND YOUR JAP TART THINK YOU'RE HOT SHIT. He sent it anonymously, but John knew it was from him – and, after confronting him, left the Cavendish house with Yoko.

"I'm a cunt," Paul confessed to Francie.

As things spiraled out of control, Paul realized he'd made a terrible mistake, moving Francie into Cavendish. When Peter Asher's secretary Chris O'Dell came by, he asked her, "How can I get rid of her?"

Get rid of her he did. Francie flew home a few days later, courtesy of Apple, leaving her movie treatment to languish in a stack of unread submissions.

And while the entire Francie situation was unfolding, Maggie was still there in the background. Paul's response to the Francie debacle and Jane's evacuation of Cavendish was to take Maggie on holiday at Sardinia. It was during that trip that he began writing "The Back Seat of My Car", a song that would eventually make its way onto his solo album *Ram*.

Underscoring just how lost he was, Paul broached the subject of marriage to Maggie in Sardinia.

"One day when we were coming out of the sea, and Paul said, 'What would you think about getting married?' I gave some flip answer like 'You never know what may happen.'"

And on the last day of their getaway, a photographer got a picture of them walking through town. They returned to London to find the picture in Sunday People, with the banner PAUL McCARTNEY'S NEW GIRLFRIEND.

And with that, the affair faded to nothing. Realizing how lost he was, Paul set his sights elsewhere.

"Dear Prudence"

Once again John manages to surprise everyone who thought they had him figured out. After the years of misogyny, confession and self-loathing he'd served up, album after album, he slips gently into the first few minutes of the *White Album* with the purest, most innocent song he's ever written.

It's not a song about a relationship. It's only autobiographical in that it does describe an actual event – but a person-to-person event, not a romantic or sexual encounter. And yet... it's very much a love song – or, at least, a loving song – and tells us a great deal about John himself, things we're relieved to learn.

"Dear Prudence" was "written in India," John told *Playboy* in 1980, during the Beatles' excursion to Rishikesh, where they studied meditation with the Maharishi Mahesh Yogi. It was "a song about Mia Farrow's sister, who seemed to go slightly barmy, meditating too long, and couldn't come out of the little hut that we were livin' in. They selected me and George to try and bring her out because she would trust us...No one was to know that sooner or later she was to go completely berserk, under the care of Maharishi Mahesh Yogi. All the people around were very worried about the girl because she was going insane. So, we sang to her."

Dear Prudence, won't you come out to play?
Dear Prudence, greet the brand new day
The sun is up, the sky is blue
It's beautiful, and so are you

Dear Prudence, open up your eyes
Dear Prudence, see the sunny skies
The wind is low, the birds will sing
That you are part of everything...

Prudence's isolation had stretched to three weeks, prompting John to speculate that she was "trying to reach God quicker than anyone else."

The American flautist Paul Horn, also in attendance, later said that she went catatonic, and didn't recognize her own brother.

Farrow later denied it. "I'd been meditating since 1966 and had tried to get on the course in 1967, so it was like a dream come true for me," she said. "Being on that course was more important than anything in the world. I was very focused on getting in as much meditation as possible, so that I could gain enough experience to teach it myself. I knew that I must have stuck out because I would always rush straight back to my room after lectures and meals so that I could meditate...John, George and Paul would all want to sit around jamming and having a good time and I'd be flying into my room. They were all serious about what they were doing but they just weren't as fanatical as me. The song that John wrote was just saying, 'Come out and play with us. Come out and have fun.'"

The Scottish pop star Donovan was also in attendance, and taught John the gentle style of fingerpicking that John plays in the song.

Though John jammed on the song with Donovan and Mike Love of the Beach Boys, who were part of the meditation course, he never played it for Prudence.

"At the end of the course, just as they were leaving, he mentioned that they had written a song about me," Farrow recalled, "but I didn't hear it until it came out on the album. I was flattered. It was a beautiful thing to have done."

Tim Riley speculated that the song is "about sexual awakening, the heady euphoria of natural pleasures wooed by a sublime musical arc." He went on to say, "nowhere else does he sound as composed as he does here, as infatuated with the innocence he's singing about ... It counts amongst Lennon's finest songs."

Recorded at Trident Studios, rather than Abbey Road, "Dear Prudence" was recorded August 28-30, 1968. Ringo had temporarily quit the band, so Paul sat in on drums.

Breaking Up is Hard to Do: Paul and Jane

The Francie Schwartz Affair had introduced two hard but certain truths into Paul and Jane's relationship: 1) Paul wasn't worthy of Jane, and 2) Jane wasn't a suitably compatible partner for Paul, even if he had been worthy.

On the one hand, their five-year relationship had survived Paul's endless whining on platinum vinyl about Jane's refusal to give up her career and be ever at his side, culminating in the announcement of their engagement announcement on Christmas Day, 1967; on the other, Paul's side gigs with Francie and Maggie McGivern were, under those circumstances, shameful, despicable, and inexcusable. It was a blatant, glaring sign that he wasn't an honest, forthright man ready to make a real commitment to a woman.

Then again, though Jane clearly loved Paul far more than Paul loved Jane, her career simply wasn't compatible with his. Even if he hadn't been a cad, had been utterly faithful and devoted, he'd still have been unable to be there for her in the way that she needed. Two people utterly dedicated to careers as artists that keep them on the road, constantly going in different directions, face the trials of Sisyphus: one or the other or both will inevitably be crushed.

Paul and Jane needed the same thing: partners with careers more flexible than their own.

After the Francie Incident, Paul and Jane had met and attempted to work things out. It could be that this effort was perfunctory; there's no way to know for sure.

What is known is that Jane ended their engagement, and their five-year relationship, in exactly the style Paul deserved, after what he'd done: she announced it on live TV, without warning him ahead of time.

It happened on a BBC talk show, *Dee Time*, a show that typically featured light entertainment. Appearing as a guest, she told the show's host, Simon Dee, that "I haven't broken it off, but it's finished.

"I know it sounds corny, but we still see each other and love each other, but it hasn't worked out," she said. "Perhaps we'll be childhood sweethearts and meet again and get married when we're about 70."

That had to be tough to hear, but at least she was gracious in her summation.

Paul responded in kind: "We had a good relationship," he said later. "Even with touring, there were enough occasions to keep a reasonable relationship going. To tell the truth, the women at that time got sidelined.

"Once or twice we talked about getting married, and plans were afoot but I don't know, something made me nervous about the whole thing. It just never settled with me, and as that's very important for me, things must feel comfortable for me, I think it's a pretty good gauge if you're lucky enough. You're not always lucky enough, but if they can feel comfortable then there's something very special about that feeling. I hadn't quite managed to be able to get it with Jane."

The truth is that Paul's crimes against Jane and their relationship were inexcusable. He was a cad. A bounder. A snake. An asshole. He got what he deserved. Jane had dodged a bullet, and had definitely made the right call, for both of them.

But even if he hadn't been that guy, it's hard to believe their relationship could have worked. Jane was Paul's muse, but she had a muse of her own, and it wasn't Paul – and Paul is on record denying that he's really into threesomes.

Still, the whole thing signaled to Paul that he needed to make some changes. It was time to man up, to stop his endless tomcatting. And he needed a more flexible partner, someone whose career and lifestyle would not only mesh well with his, but nudge him toward a healthier path.

He'd already met her. He just hadn't thought it through yet.

"Ob-La-Di, Ob-La-Da"

As the *White Album* was taking shape in 1968, Paul had met Linda Eastman, and his prospects for marriage to Jane were very much down the drain. Spinning up material for the new album, and having waxed eloquent on his ideas about long-term bliss in "When I'm Sixty-Four", it's no great leap to the setting of "Ob-La-Di, Ob-La-Da", an unbearably cheerful group portrait of what Paul conceives of as a deliriously happy family. Considering Linda as a possible partner in his desired bliss leads almost bee-line into the domicile of Desmond and Molly Jones.

The song opens by introducing the two, then proceeds to their engagement:

Desmond takes a trolley to the jeweler's store
Buys a twenty-carat golden ring
Takes it back to Molly waiting at the door
And as he gives it to her she begins to sing

Ob-la-di, ob-la-da, life goes on, bra
La-la, how the life goes on...

This slice of heaven, Paul's actual dream for himself, only gets better with babies:

In a couple of years, they have built a home-sweet-home
With a couple of kids running in the yard
Of Desmond and Molly Jones

In an interesting twist, it's Molly rather than Desmond who's the musician in the family – Desmond "has a barrow in the marketplace." But more interesting still, even though "in the evening she still sings it with the band," the focus of the Joneses is family, even over music. This is Paul's future – his "happy ever after" in the song – with Linda and the kids that will run in their yard, touring the world with Wings.

The delightfully airy music behind the cheery portraits will bring a smile to almost anyone, but it was counter-intuitively laborious getting there. In Paul's head, the song was a muscled ska-fest – Jamaica through a fuzz pedal. Three days of effort got the band nowhere, until finally John, in inebriated frustration, sat down at the piano, shouting *"This is how the fucking song should go!"* and pounded it out with the cheery music-hall vibe that Paul should have thought of in the first place. Martin brought in cheery sax players, and the *White Album* now had what is by far its most commercial track. But despite this, the band vetoed Paul's push to have it released as a single; he'd pissed them off too badly at that point.

The tortured sessions occurred July 8, 9, 11 and 15 of 1968.

Apple Scruffs

Early in the Beatles' career, teenage girls began standing constant watch on the sidewalks outside their homes, outside Abbey Road andApple headquarters, outside anywhere they happened to be, standing vigil in hopes of seeing one of their idols and grabbing a moment of their time.

The Beatles and the Apple staff grew used to the scruffs after a time. Ringo, for instance, would greet them as he trotted up the steps of Apple headquarters: "Hello girls, busy day?"

But from time to time, this bizarre dedication paid off. During the recording of an early version of John's "Across the Universe", for instance, Paul went outside and recruited two scruffs, Lizzie Bravo and Gayleen Pease, to sing backing vocals on the song.

When Paul wrote "Blackbird", he tried the song out on some scruffs outside his London home, sitting in the window and serenading them:

Blackbird singing in the dead of night
Take these broken wings and learn to fly...

The scruffs, of course, were not fans of the women the Beatles actually chose to be with. In an odd contradiction, head scruff Margo Stevens[40] would try to warn Paul, on a night when he was in his Cavendish Avenue home with secret girlfriend Francie Schwartz, that Jane had arrived and was on her way into the house.

Several scruffs broke into Paul's Cavendish home when he was away in 1968, stealing a pair of his trousers. They proceeded to take turns wearing them. They also stole a framed picture, but later returned it.[41] Their exploits were immortalized in a section of the famous *Abbey Road* medley, "She Came in Through the Bathroom Window".[42]

---

[40]Stevens was present at the "Blackbird" serenade, and actually attended Paul and Linda's wedding.

[41]Margo Stevens brokered the return of the photo.

Apple lieutenant Derek Taylor would later describe the scruffs as "very Zen," commenting that he would invite them into Apple headquarters when they were caught in the rain. They would decline, he said: "The strange thing was they were happy there. They didn't want to be on the inside."

A scruff named Carol Bedford actually wrote a memoir, published in 1985 – *Waiting for the Beatles: An Apple Scruff's Story*.

George, who coined the term, immortalized them in song, post-Beatles, in his tribute song "Apple Scruffs" on the album *All Things Must Pass*:[43]

> *In the fog and in the rain*
> *Through the pleasures and the pain*
> *On the step outside you stand*
> *With your flowers in your hand, my Apple Scruffs*
>
> *While the years, they come and go*
> *Now, your love must surely show me*
> *That beyond all time and space*
> *We're together face to face, my Apple Scruffs*
>
> *Apple Scruffs, Apple Scruffs*
> *How I love you, how I love you*

---

[42]The scruff who led the raid, Emma Eldridge, confessed in 2014.

[43]Per biographer Alan Clayson, the song was "the most intrinsically valuable if belated recognition of a vigil soon to end with adulthood [for the scruffs] and the realization that the Beatles as a 1960s myth would long outlive the mere mortals that constituted its *dramatis personae*".

"Happiness is a Warm Gun"

It is no surprise that the Beatles' most overtly sexual song was written by John. And it makes sense that he couldn't have written it before Yoko had come into his life.

"Happiness is a Warm Gun", by far John's most inventive track on the *White Album*, is on the one hand an overt homage to Yoko – and is, on the other, a veritable sex manual.

The song's three sources were, as with "Walrus", wildly disparate. The first was a brainstorming session at Peter Asher's home between John, Derek Taylor, Neil Aspinall and Pete Shotton while they were tripping.

"John said he had written half a song and wanted us to toss out phrases while Neil wrote them down," said Taylor. "First of all, he wanted to know how to describe a girl who was really smart and I remembered a phrase of my father's which was 'she's not a girl who misses much.'"

Then came

> *Like a lizard on a window pane*
> *She's well acquainted with the touch of the velvet hand*
> *The man in the crowd with multi-colored mirrors on his hobnail boots*
> *Lying with his eyes while his hands are busy working overtime*

...and others. John managed to weave these random sentences into a coherent narrative about a man obsessed with a fascinating, disturbing woman. Kenneth Womack's take:

"She's become jaded by her very own shrewdness, by the breadth of her own experience," he wrote. "John's description of the character's prurient eroticism - 'She's well-acquainted with the touch of the velvet hand / Like a lizard on a window pane' - finds his poetry at its salacious best. She likes soft touch alright, but only when it's well-tempered by the scaly raw urgency of human sexuality. Her sleazy voyeuristic counterpart is 'the man in the crowd with the multicolored mirrors / on his hobnail boots'. He masturbates publicly - 'lying with his eyes while his hands are busy working overtime' - before Lennon's psychosexual nether world dissolves before our very ears."

The second source was Yoko. Whether she is also the woman in the song's first section isn't altogether clear, but her presence in the second is unquestionable. From "I need a fix..." through "Mother Superior jump the gun," he's announcing his passion for her, in excruciating detail. This was actually the first part of the song John wrote, and his original demo contains nothing more. (It was in his quest for more content for the song that John turned to his acid buddies at Asher's home.)

Then there's the warm gun.

"A gun magazine was sitting around, and the cover was the picture of a smoking gun," he told *Playboy* in 1980, referring to an issue of American Rifleman that George Martin showed him. "The title of the article, which I never read, was 'Happiness Is a Warm Gun'." The phrase is, of course, a play on "Happiness is a warm puppy," from Charles Schultz's cartoon strip Peanuts.

"I thought, 'What a fantastic, insane thing to say.; A warm gun means you've just shot something."

John referred to the three sections of "Happiness" as "The Dirty Old Man," "The Junkie," and "The Gunman."

"When John put it all together, it created a series of layers of images," Taylor said later. "It was like a whole mess of color."

The line "I need a fix" led many to speculate that John was writing about heroin, which John repeatedly denied. He bluntly admitted to *Playboy* that "Mother Superior" was Yoko and the "gun" she was jumping was a sexual metaphor.[44]

"...the most purely Lennonian aspect of 'Happiness is a Warm Gun' is its extreme ambiguity," wrote Ian Macdonald. "From an initial mood of depression, it ascends through irony, self-destructive despair, and obscurely renewed energy to a finale that wrests exhausted fulfillment from anguish. Grippingly uneasy listening, the track's tense blend of sarcasm and sincerity stays unresolved until its final detumescent downbeat."

John and Paul both named "Happiness" as their favorite track on the *White Album*, and George and Ringo later agreed. And on

---

[44] John actually addressed Yoko by name in the original demo.

top of that, the BBC banned the song. All told, that's unqualified praise.

The band played through 95 takes on the nights of September 23-26, 1968, to get the song down.

For the Love of Pattie

While John, Paul and Ringo had all proposed marriage to women who were pregnant with their babies, George had married Pattie without that motivation – though, ironically, both really wanted children.

As the Beatles slaved away on the *White Album*, more than two years had passed and they hadn't managed it, which disappointed them both. Their lives weren't exactly empty – the Beatles' decision to give up touring had given all of them a much more flexible lifestyle, filled with travel and culture and adventure, when the band wasn't in the studio – but there was a corresponding increase in drug and alcohol intake (Pattie developed kidney trouble at one point), and children might have been a healthier investment of George and Pattie's time.

Pattie wasn't the only important person George had met in 1964; he'd also bonded with a brilliant British guitarist with a gift for the blues named Eric Clapton. And as George went through his usual Sisyphian struggle to get John and Paul to take his songs seriously and give them their best efforts, it occurred to him to bring Clapton in to give a much-needed boost to a particular song the band had started laying down: "While My Guitar Gently Weeps".

The outcome of that decision is well-known to hundreds of millions; the song is one of the best-loved in the Beatles canon, and is probably one of George's top two or three songs written as a Beatle.

The increased presence of Clapton in the Beatles circle had an unexpected consequence. He fell in love with Pattie.

He began to flirt with her whenever they were in common company, which no one took seriously – least of all Pattie, who knew Clapton to be one of her husband's closest friends. George didn't either, for that matter.

Still, the attention had an impact: "It was hard not to be flattered when I caught him staring at me or when he chose to sit beside me or complimented me on what I was wearing," she wrote in her autobiography. "Those were all things that George no longer did."

Not long after, she received an anonymous love letter. Well, not entirely anonymous; it was signed *E*. And not long after, Clapton called her and asked if she'd received it. She was stunned and uncomfortable.

"It was the most passionate letter anyone had ever written to me and it put our relationship on a different footing," she wrote. "It made the flirtation all the more exciting and dangerous. But as far as I was concerned, it was just flirtation."

Perhaps, but the timing couldn't have been worse. The increased drug use was taking a serious toll on the marriage.

"That whole period was insane," she wrote. "Those last years of marriage were fueled by alcohol and cocaine. The drugs froze George's emotions and hardened his heart."

Clapton had formed a Pepper-like alternate identity band, Derek and the Dominos, and was working on that album when he finally made his move. Inviting Pattie over to his home, he played a tape of a new song he'd written for the album. A song about his unrequited passion for Pattie. One of the greatest rock songs ever written.

"Layla".

He played it for her, and she was moved beyond belief.

"My first thought was, 'Oh, God, everyone's going to know who this is,' she wrote. 'I felt uncomfortable that he was pushing me in a direction I wasn't certain I wanted to go. But the song got the better of me, with the realization that I had inspired such passion and such creativity. I could resist no longer."

Later that evening, they both attended a party at Robert Stigwood's home. George showed up and found the two of them in the garden, holding hands.

"I have to tell you, man, that I'm in love with your wife," Clapton blurted out to George, to Pattie's horror.

Furious, George turned to Pattie and demanded to know, "Are you going with him or are you coming with me?"

She was going with George. For the moment.

"Don't Pass Me By"

It took him more than six years, but Ringo *finally* got a song he'd written on a Beatles album! And it was a love song – more or less.

He'd written the song long before, presenting it to them way back when he joined the band, in August 1962.

He relished it:

"I wrote 'Don't Pass Me By' when I was sitting round at home," he said. "I was fiddling with the piano – I just bang away – and then if a melody comes and some words, I just have to keep going. It was great to get my first song down, one that I had written. It was a very exciting time for me and everyone was really helpful, and recording that crazy violinist was a thrilling moment."

Of the track, John said Ringo had "composed it himself, in a fit of lethargy."

The song is actually straightforward country rock, with a bluegrass fiddle added by jazz bassist Jack Fallon. It is warm and goofy and ridiculous and fun, and *White Album* aficionados either love it to death or can't stand it.

The singer is making a personal appeal to a woman he desperately doesn't want to lose:

I listen for your footsteps, coming up the drive
Listen for your footsteps, but they don't arrive
Waiting for your knock, dear, on my old front door
I don't hear it, does it mean you don't love me anymore?

Don't pass me by, don't make me cry, don't make me blue
'Cause you know, darlin', I love only you...

This all seems appropriately empty-headed, but Ringo's true wit and passive awareness manage to creep out:

I'm sorry that I doubted you, I was so unfair
You were in a car crash, and you lost your hair

Fallon's fiddle wanders around with delightful randomness. The barstool-and-beer pulse of Paul's piano creates a sing-along vibe, and Ringo indulges in no less than all manner of ornamental percussion, breaking out a cowbell (of course), congas, maracas – even sleigh bells.

And what does this song tell us about Ringo as a man? A lover? A husband? Not a damn thing. And that's kind of the point.

The song was appropriately covered two decades later by the Georgia Satellites, an American southern rock band who went out of their way to cultivate a façade as illiterate rednecks. It was a perfect wedding of artist and material.

Simple as the song is, and as basic as the rendering of it seems to be, it consumed four days of studio time to complete – June 5, 6, 12 and 22, 1968. Odder still is the fact that Ringo and Paul are the only two Beatles appearing, plus Fallon.

You Say You Want a (Sexual) Revolution

Above, we excoriated the Beatles for their misogynistic missteps. Below, we praise them for their emergent feminism.

To fully appreciate that emergence, it's helpful to place oneself firmly in the context of the early Sixties. As Kenneth Womack expresses it,

"Rock 'n' roll, or even popular music, [was] often highly gendered and sexist. It certainly was paternalistic in the Sixties and prior, in terms of songs being directed at women as objects, women as needing to be 'counseled' about love, [or] it was about coming on to them, even if it was just something innocent and romantic..."

Innocent and romantic are certainly words that can be applied to the Beatles' early songs. We've already noted, in our 'pronoun' analysis above, that the big meta-hook of Beatles lyricism is that the singer is directly addressing the female listener: *I'm singing to you!* Though this wasn't unique to the Beatles, they were certainly the first to platform their entire musical presentation on that technique.

Even then, when their songs were largely themed on courtship and Happy-in-Love, there's a submissive quality in their lyrical expression that separates them from the rock 'n' roll attitude that Womack describes - the singer is presenting himself for the woman's approval, hoping to demonstrate his worthiness:

This boy wouldn't mind the pain
Would always feel the same
If this boy gets you back again...

In this new perspective, it's the woman's simple presence that the singer treasures, over and above her affections or her sexuality:

I don't need to hug or hold you tight
I just want to dance with you all night

In this world there's nothing I would rather do
'Cause I'm happy just to dance with you

John goes for broke in "It Won't Be Long", where he actually goes so far as to declare his own helplessness:

Every night when everybody has fun
Here I am sitting all on my own
I'll be good like I know I should
You're coming home, you're coming home

And, more revealing still,

It won't be long 'til I belong to you

I belong to you... rather than the other way around.

Even more telling is the man-to-man tone of "She Loves You", where the singer is an observer, rather than a lover, telling one of his pals to get his act together after mistreating his girlfriend:

You know it's up to you
I think it's only fair
Pride can hurt you too
Apologize to her

"This is a long way from groin-centered rock," writes columnist Karen Hooper.

In putting a song like this on Top 40 radio, the Beatles are sending out a new take on relationships, in which guys need to man up and treat their women right, and accept the responsibility that goes with the privilege. That in itself was revolutionary at the time.

Soon after, Womack says, the Beatles' covert feminism took another step forward:

"...the Beatles very consciously in 1965 began to change their tone," he said. "They created a very specific type of female character who would think for herself and did not need a man. And that is revelatory, really. We have many songs that begin to appear at that point that are highly progressive about women living their own interests and aims and pleasure, as opposed to serving some undefinable other. It's pretty exciting stuff."

We've already noted the Women of *Rubber Soul* – John's clandestine lover in "Norwegian Wood", the soul-crushing antagonist in "Girl" - as women empowered. There's also the woman in "Ticket to Ride", whose independence and agency are a tremendous torment to John, as his love goes unrequited. These characters exist in the Beatles landscape to make more real and relevant their commentary on love and relationship, and (whether intentionally or not) present themselves more honestly.

This new woman appears again and again – in "Drive My Car", "Day Tripper" - relentlessly underscoring feminine independence, a portrait of a woman who doesn't need a man to make her way in the world. One of her most telling incarnations surfaces on *Pepper*, in the form of the teenage girl who slips out the back door of her parents' home, willing to forfeit a life of ease for a self-directed one.

But it wasn't just the lyrics and the characters they brought to life. The Beatles themselves promoted a new and different attitude about gender relations, simply in the way they presented themselves. This began with their appreciation of girl-group music, according to writer Cameron Hilditch:

"The Rolling Stones wanted to be Muddy Waters or Howlin' Wolf," he wrote. "The Beatles wanted to be the Shirelles or the Ronettes."

That's a very telling insight, because the songs of the Shirelles and the Ronettes position the woman as supplicant and the man as having the power in the relationship. Per Hilditch, when the Beatles stepped into that dynamic, the gender reversal changes everything:

"In girl-group love songs of the Sixties, there is a traditional division of masculine and feminine gender roles in matters of courtship," he writes. "The singer (a woman) is an adoring onlooker, devoid of sexual agency but hoping against hope that the object of the song (a man) will choose her and treat her well... The man to whom she is singing is the one with all the choices, all the power, all the prerogatives, as society in the Fifties and early Sixties basically dictated. The Beatles completely reverse this dynamic. They put themselves in the place of the helpless, passive supplicant and bestow all of the sexual agency in the relationship on the girl. This dynamic is at work most explicitly in their recorded covers of girl-group songs, such as the Marvelettes' 'Please, Mister Postman'. Lennon changes the noun from 'boyfriend' to 'girlfriend,' and, in doing so, upends centuries of traditional gender dynamics."

The result, Hilditch argues, is that "the Beatles told girls that it was okay to be the one making decisions and taking action when it comes to sex and relationships. They also gave boys permission to be more vulnerable and to ask for love and affection from the opposite sex. As a result of Lennon and McCartney's role-reversal with the Shirelles and the Ronettes, they wrote songs in which men are more feminine and women are more masculine, in terms of how the two genders relate to one another, than had been the case in pop music before."

They were, he concluded, "deconstructing the crew-cut, buttoned-down, Eisenhower-era models of masculinity and femininity."

"The Beatles helped feminize the culture," wrote Martin King in *Men, Masculinity and The Beatles*. "The implications of the Beatles' relatively androgynous appearance had a far more profound effect on sexual and women's liberation than anyone could have guessed at the time. [They] challenged the definition that existed during their time of what it meant to be a man. This ultimately allowed them to help change the way men feel and look."

All this adds up, in Hilditch's formulation, to revolution. The bolstering of female sexual agency and the creation of safe zones for male vulnerability and supplication put the lie to the patriarchal hierarchy of love and sex that had dominated Western culture seemingly for eons. No longer was the man in charge; no longer was the female there for his pleasure and reproductive legacy. Love is a two-way street, they declared, and sex is as much a pleasure-oriented domain for women as for men.

"The music of the Beatles divorces sex from any necessary connection with child-rearing and monogamy and pairs it with the exhilarating romantic ethic of the courtly-love tradition," Hilditch wrote. "They took the material conditions of the sexual revolution (the invention of effective birth control) and used it as a jumping-off point for renovating the relationship between the sexes. Not that any of this was deliberate, of course; no one, least of all the Beatles themselves, could have imagined that their music would have any kind of broad social influence, let alone that it would become the world's favorite thing. But it is, nevertheless, what happened. There isn't a single corner or facet of pop culture that hasn't been affected by the way that John Lennon and Paul McCartney sang about girls."

This is not to say, of course, that the Beatles themselves actually lived up to the gender-balanced idealism of their songs. Womack felt that they certainly didn't.

"I think [Paul and John] were very aware that they were these kinds of contradictions, that they were talking out of both sides of their mouths," he wrote. "Their own actions hadn't caught up with their intellectual abilities. But I do think they were conscious of the fact that they were hypocrites. I think it actually makes them more interesting that they're both victimizers, to a certain extent, and wanting to be better. They are very fractured vessels, but they knew enough to believe it was important and to use their massive bully pulpit or bullhorn, which is still about the biggest one in history, to talk about these things."

In any case, the Sexual Revolution rolled forward, feminism swept the West, and we live in a very different world today because of those transitional years. And the Beatles were certainly there at the center of it all.

"The Beatles may not have invented birth control," wrote Hilditch, "but they did invent the self-image of the young people of the Sixties who used it. They provided these young people with music and lyrics that acclimatized them to the new sexual technology and taught them how to use it to relate to each other in a new and exciting way. That's why the girls in Shea Stadium lost their minds, their dignity, and any sense of self-restraint at the sight of Paul McCartney, but probably hadn't a clue as to who invented the Pill."

"Julia"

After the innocence of "Prudence" and the lusty cacophony of "Happiness", John tells us how he *really* feels.

"Julia", written in India with Donovan's support, was a song John had been needing to write all his life – and was yet another song he couldn't have possibly written, pre-Yoko.

Many would say that this obvious truth owes to Yoko's presence in the song - "ocean child" - but the reality underneath is that John couldn't fully process his long-ago loss of his mother until he had found a way to restore at least a part of what he had lost. Yoko, who in many ways became a mother-figure to John, represented that long-needed restoration.

"He told me he wanted to write a song about his mother," Donovan recalled in an interview with *Vulture*. "He said, 'Donovan, you're the king of children's songs. Can you help me?... I want to write a song about the childhood that I never really had with my mother.' He asked me to help him with the images that he could use in lyrics for a song about this subject. So I said, 'Well, when you think of the song, where do you imagine yourself?' And John said, 'I'm at a beach and I'm holding hands with my mother and we're walking together.' And I helped him with a couple of lines, 'Seashell eyes / windy smile' – for the Lewis Carroll/Alice in Wonderland feel that John loved so much"

Another co-author was Lebonese poet Kahlil Gibran, whose 1927 book of proverbs *Sand and Foam* gave John part of the first lyrics in the song:

Half of what I say is meaningless
But I say it just to reach you, Julia

John's sudden loss of his mother was an ancient remnant of memory as he approached his 30th birthday, but it was the pivotal moment of his life: everything he had experienced, lived through since had been in one way or another a consequence of that horrific event.[45] Now he was going to confront it, as all the world listened.

"'Julia', with which Yoko helped, expiates Lennon's tortured devotion to his mother," Ian Macdonald wrote. "In the incantatory repeated notes of its intro, the song suggests an offering to an ancestral spirit: an attempt to break an obsession by commending the supplicant's new earthly love in the hope of a blessing. The heart of this ritual – the transfer of Lennon's love from Julia to Yoko – is its ten-bar middle where a quasi-oriental scale implies that the accompanying image (*Her hair of floating sky is shimmering*) applies to both women: Julia in his boyhood memory, Yoko in his present and future thoughts."

His mother was the template for womanhood that both inspired him and screwed him up. "'Julia' illuminates the mystery that the image of woman represents for John," wrote Tim Riley. "The grief of loss and the insufferable longing he still feels for his mother better explain his earlier heartache songs – their jealousy and intimidation – as the result of some traumatic inner conflict."

When I cannot sing my heart
I can only speak my mind
Julia
Julia, sleeping sand, silent cloud
Touch me
So I sing a song of love
Julia

"Arguably his most powerful and fully realized composition... ['Julia'] finds him examining the nature and beauty of his new relationship with Yoko through the auspices of Julia's memory," per Kenneth Womack. "It's an astounding achievement that Lennon never equals, especially given the song's remarkable personal and musical significance in his life."

---

[45]His close friendship with Paul, for example, became one of the most consequential relationships in music history – and owed much to the fact that their mutual loss of their mothers had been a large factor in their original bonding. And Ian Macdonald points out that his endless violent, angry relationships with women over the years were largely a product of his comparison of them to Julia.

"Lennon's most child-like and self-revealing song, 'Julia' is almost too personal for public consumption," Macdonald wrote. "To a great extent, Julia Lennon was her son's muse. Once he had rid his soul of grief for her, his creativity forfeited its pressure and, during his more reconciled final decade, his output lost most of the edge and forcefulness it displayed at its fundamentally unhappy zenith in the mid-Sixties."

Recorded on October 13, 1968 – the final *White Album* track to be recorded - "Julia" is John's only completely solo performance on any Beatles album.

The Beatles Guide to Love & Sex

1969:

All I Have to Do is Think of Her

From Me to You: Pattie's Greatest Hits

Pattie Boyd Harrison Clapton – possibly the most written-about woman in all of rock.

As recorded above, Pattie became the third Beatle Wife on January 21, 1966, two years into their relationship. In the interim, George became the second Beatle to write a song directly to his partner: "I Need You", on the album *Help!*

"I Need You" was George's second successful songwriting effort for the band (the first was "Don't Bother Me", from *With the Beatles*). John gave him a hand with it, working on the song at John's Weybridge home on the day of Ringo and Maureen's wedding – February 11, 1965.

There are two interesting things going on in the song. The first is George holding Pattie up as his shelter in the storm, against the exhausting onslaught of Beatlemania, which he more than the others found intolerable. The second is found in lyrics that subtly refer to a brief separation between the two, before the song was written:

Oh, yes, you told me
You don't want my lovin' any more

Please come on back to me
I'm lonely as can be

Pattie had left George briefly because she was fed up with the band's endless roiling ocean of female fans.[46]

Next came "If I Needed Someone", which George produced for *Rubber Soul* (see page 92). George wrote the song for Pattie, though it reads as unsettlingly ambiguous:

---

[46] A musically interesting feature of the song is that it represents the first use of a guitar volume pedal in a Beatles recording.

Carve your number on my wall
And maybe you will get a call from me

Had you come some other day
Then it might not have been like this

Somewhat patronizing in tone, he's sounding like a true Liverpudlian man of his times. But next comes:

But you see now I'm too much in love

Tim Riley calls the song "qualified flirtation."

"It's All Too Much", from the soundtrack of *Yellow Submarine*, was inspired by George's first acid trip in March 1965, an experience he shared with Pattie and the other Beatles and their wives. Though he includes the line, *With your long blonde hair and your eyes of blue*, nominally a reference to Pattie, that line in fact occurs in the McCoys tune "Sorrow".

"For You Blue" was the last Beatles song released that Pattie inspired, but was in fact recorded earlier, during the January 1969 *Get Back* sessions that became the belated swansong album *Let It Be*. An unlikely country-blues tune with an exuberant tone, it unabashedly declares George's love for Pattie:

Because you're sweet and lovely, girl, I love you
Because you're sweet and lovely, girl, it's true
I love you more than ever, girl, I do

I want you in the morning, girl, I love you
I want you at the moment I feel blue
I'm living every moment, girl, for you

Beatles musicologist Alan Pollack describes the song as "unusually unmuddled romantic euphoria."

Finally, there "Something", George's uncontested masterpiece, and the second-most-covered song in the Beatles catalog (behind "Yesterday").[47]

Though George was noncommittal in interviews about his inspiration for the song, Pattie wrote in her autobiography that "he told me in a matter-of-fact way that he had written it for me. I thought it was beautiful and it turned out to be the most successful song he ever wrote."[48]

Beautiful, certainly. It's impossible not to think so...

Something in the way she moves
Attracts me like no other lover
Something in the way she woos me
I don't want to leave her now
You know I believe and how

Something in the way she knows
And all I have to do is think of her
Something in the things she shows me
I don't want to leave her now
You know I believe and how

And then there's Eric Clapton.

The legendary blues/rock guitarist, called "God" by his millions of fans, met George in 1964 and their friendship culminated in his signature work on George's *White Album* gem, "While My Guitar Gently Weeps" - a Beatles first. Eric would go on to form Cream, Blind Faith and Derek and the Dominos before launching a decades-long solo career as one of rock's true masters. And his friendship with George persisted through the latter's death in 2001.[49]

After his *White Album* appearance, Eric took notice of Pattie – and sent her a letter, signed "E", in hopes of beginning a

---

[47]It was also declared by both John and Paul to be the best track on *Abbey Road*.

[48]In *Wonderful Tonight: George Harrison, Eric Clapton, and Me*.

[49]We'd be remiss if we didn't note Clapton's tribute to his friend, *Concert for George* in 2002, which united Paul, Ringo, Billy Preston, Dhani Harrison, Jeff Lynne, Monty Python, Ravi Shankar and many others at the Royal Albert Hall for one of the greatest memorial concerts ever performed.

relationship with her. By this time, her marriage to George had begun to fray, and she later confessed to being "intrigued." Eric's pursuit of her became obsessive, and by the time the Beatles were truly over – December 31, 1970, when their legal partnership was dissolved – he had written his passion for her into song, with no less than *four* Pattie-inspired tracks on his Derek and the Dominos supergroup album *Layla and Other Assorted Love Songs*.

"Layla", the title track, is a sonic and lyrical maelstrom of emotional torment.[50] It is Clapton prostrate for all the world to see:

Let's make the best of the situation
Before I finally go insane
Please don't say I'll never find a way
And tell me all my love's in vain

Layla, you've got me on my knees
Layla, I'm begging, darling please
Layla, darling won't you ease my worried mind

The inspiration for "Bell Bottom Blues" can be taken at face value: Pattie asked Eric to bring her a pair of bell bottom jeans from the United States, and this is what popped out:

Do you want to see me crawl across the floor to you
Do you want to hear me beg you to take me back
I'd gladly do it because I don't want to fade away
Give me one more day, please
I don't want to fade away
In your heart I want to stay

Not far afield of the sentiments of "Layla"; emotional torment, indulged to the fullest.

---

[50]"Layla" is #27 on *Rolling Stone*'s 500 Greatest Songs of All Time list; the acoustic version, performed live on MTV, won the Grammy Award for Best Rock Song in 1993.

Lesser known are "Why Has Love Got to Be So Sad" and "I Looked Away".

From the former:

Got to find me a way
To take me back to yesterday
How can I ever hope to forget you?
Won't you show me a place
Where I can hide my lonely face?
I know you're going to break my heart if I let you
Why does love got to be so sad?

And from the latter (the album's opening track):

It came as no surprise to me
That she'd leave me in misery
It seemed like only yesterday
She made a vow that she'd never walk away
She took my hand
To try to make me understand
That she would always be there
But I looked away
And she ran away from me today
I'm such a lonely man

No question, Eric was one messed-up guy that year.

How did Pattie feel about being the object of this torrent of romantic angst?

She and Eric had a secret meeting at a South Kensington flat in London where the Dominos had moved. He played the newly-recorded "Layla" for her, several times, on a tape machine. She thought the song was "the most powerful, moving song I had ever heard."

At the same time, she thought, "Oh, god, everyone's going to know who this is. I felt uncomfortable that he was pushing me in a direction I wasn't certain I wanted to go. But the song got the better of me, with the realization that I had inspired such passion and such creativity. I could resist no longer."

And then Eric gave her a "Something" - a timeless romantic ballad that would become an instant classic:
"Wonderful Tonight".[51]

We go to a party
And every one turns to see
This beautiful lady
Who's walking around with me
And then she asks me
"Do you feel all right?"
And I say, "Yes, I feel wonderful tonight"

I feel wonderful because I see the love light in your eyes
Then the wonder of it all is that you just don't realize
How much I love you...

This one was as literal as could be. "One night, Eric and I were going out, but I couldn't decide what to wear. I was taking a very long time to do my makeup and hair, putting on one dress, then another and another, throwing them all in a pile on the floor. Poor Eric had been ready for hours and was waiting patiently. He was so sweet – at least in the early days.

"When I finally got downstairs and asked the inevitable question, 'Do I look all right?', he played me what he'd written:

It's late in the evening
She's wondering what clothes to wear
She puts on her makeup and brushes her long blonde hair
And then she asks me, 'Do I look all right?'
And I say, 'Yes, you look wonderful tonight...'

"It was such a simple song," she wrote in her autobiography (which was titled after that song), "but so beautiful and for years it tore at me."

---

[51]From the 1977 album *Slowhand*. There would be one final Pattie song, "She's Waiting", from his 1985 album *Behind the Sun*: "My love has gone behind the sun / Since she left, the darkness has begun / The smile that used to shine on me / Is nothing more than a memory"

Putting it all together as she looked back on those years of her life, she wrote, "To have inspired Eric, and George before him, to write such music was so flattering. Yet I came to believe that although something about me might have made them put pen to paper, it was really all about them. And I think the depressions they suffered were to do with the creative process – the need that all creative people have to delve deep inside themselves to bring to the surface whatever they're creating."

"Don't Let Me Down"

By the time he got around to writing his bluesy paean to Yoko, "Don't Let Me Down", John's demons had found their place: they no longer ruled him sadistically, but neither were they expunged. Their residence in his psyche was permanent, but a truce had been negotiated – thanks to her:

Nobody ever loved me like she does
Oh, she does, yes, she does
And if somebody loved me like she do me
Oh, she do me, yes, she does

And then he pleads, begs, practically shouts,

Don't let me down, don't let me down...

And while he's at it, he addresses all that came before Yoko, tucking it away in whatever place it will now live:

I'm in love for the first time
Don't you know it's gonna last
It's a love that lasts forever
It's a love that has no past

Steven Turner pointed out that "'If I Fell' was the template for a number of songs in which [John] confessed his need for love and anxiety over being rejected." Very true; and "Don't Let Me Down" is the apex of that template's expression. The song is "...a pledge of devotion that writhes in the fear of loss," according to Tim Riley. "His first ode to Yoko is a cry of paranoia so honest and heartfelt that it strikes as deep a pathos as 'In My Life'."

Recorded during the chaotic *Get Back* sessions on January 28, 1969, "Don't Let Me Down" got two readings in the infamous Rooftop Concert two days later, but was ultimately deleted from the *Let It Be* album by its secondary producer, Phil Spector. It went on the B-side of the "Get Back" single.

"For You Blue"

In the *Get Back* sessions, George's "All Things Must Pass" had, astonishingly, not made the cut. More astonishing still, neither did "Something".

"For You Blue", a simplistic love note he wrote for Pattie in 12-bar blues, *did* make the cut, appearing on the eventual *Let It Be*.

A note in Wikipedia illuminates this puzzle: "Other commentators identify ["For You Blue"] as an inconsequential song, particularly in relation to some of the Harrison compositions that his bandmates rejected over the *Let It Be* period."

The inconsistency aside, there is really good reason for including "For You Blue" as a song of consequence in the Beatles love song story.

Because you're sweet and lovely, girl, I love you
Because you're sweet and lovely, girl, it's true
I love you more than ever, girl, I do

The last line of this first version makes the point. Consider: at the time the song was written and recorded, George and Pattie had been married three full years, and been together almost five. And he loves her more than ever. The stability of that relationship – especially compared to John's relationship with Cynthia and Paul's relationship with Jane – is kind of amazing, in context.

Consider that this stability and devotion have grown in a man who, at the time the song was recorded (January 25, 1969), *is still only a mere 25 years old*,[52] and has had every opportunity to choose from infinite romantic alternatives and leave his first true love behind, as his bandmates had done. Not only did he stick with it, he's shown here that his love has grown:

---

[52]He would soon turn 26 (on February 25, 1969).

I want you in the morning, girl, I love you
I want you at the moment, I feel blue
I'm living every moment, girl, for you

I've loved you from the moment I saw you
You looked at me and that's all you had to do
I feel it now, I hope you feel it too

"For You Blue" is a document of consequence in the Beatles love songbook because it's the first (and only) renewal of devotion after years of getting a relationship right.

And, of course, when it came to singing his love for Pattie, the best was yet to come.

Bros

As the Beatles moved beyond the *Get Back* debacle into *Abbey Road*, their final work together, they were – for the first time – all married men. *Abbey Road* would be the only album made where that was true.

John had been married before, of course, but divorced in 1968; his marriage to Yoko returned him to Married status. And Paul had, of course, finally left bachelorhood behind.

Both of those weddings had occurred in March 1969. Those were not the only things the two marriages had in common.

They occurred eight days apart - Paul and Linda on the 12th, John and Yoko on the 20th;

Both Yoko and Linda had been married before – Beatles firsts;

Both had small daughters – Heather, 6 (Linda), and Kyoko, 5 (Yoko).

Both courtships had lasted less than a year (Paul and Linda, around six months; John and Yoko, around six months). Previous Beatles premarital courtships had all lasted more than two years.

But they had more in common still.

Though Paul would remarry twice after Linda's death, history makes clear that Linda was the love he had waited for. Their marriage would endure for almost 30 years, producing three children, and take up legendary status as one of rock's most enduring.

And though John would initially have a stormy five years with Yoko, the two would settle into a peaceful and even blissful family life at the Dakota with the arrival of son Sean in 1975, until John's death in 1980.

They had been very different boys in youth, very different men in adulthood – different boyfriends, different lovers, possessed of different appetites, goals, and failings. And yet, in the end, their love lives became very much the same – happy, harmonious, and fulfilling.

"I Want You (She's So Heavy)"

"Don't Let Me Down" was as Yoko as a John song could be, or so it seemed; "I Want You (She's So Heavy)" tried to top it.

The song was not only a captivating study of sexual obsession but a musical deep-dive into the "sound" of mental anguish. It was everything John had been reaching for in "Happiness Is a Warm Gun", "I'm So Tired" and "Everybody's Got Something to Hide Except Me and My Monkey" - all *White Album* attempts to sort out his feelings.

It is fitting that the last-ever Beatles track be so generous in its innovations and experimentation. The longest actual Beatles song at 7:49, it also has the fewest lyrics (13 words total) of any Beatles song, and is the first rock album to feature, rather than simply noodle around with, the Moog synthesizer. It was the first Beatles album recorded entirely on an eight-track recorder, and the first to be recorded and mixed through a solid-state mixing console.

But it's the content of the song that matters most. Its message is simple, very straightforward:

I want you
I want you so bad
I want you
I want you so bad, it's driving me mad
It's driving me mad

All five of the song's verses are that. Over and over. Sparse though it is, it manages to pack in as much obsession and paranoia as the more articulate "Don't Let me Down".

The chorus is simpler still:

She's so heavy
Heavy, heavy, heavy

This simplicity drew some public mockery:

"On *24 Hours* they just sardonically read the 'I Want You' lyrics: 'I want you. She's so heavy,'" John recalled. "That's all is says, but to me that's a damn sight better than 'Walrus' or 'Eleanor Rigby' lyric-wise because it's a progression to me. If I want to write songs with no words or one word, then maybe that's Yoko's influence."

The song's working title was simply "I Want You" for most of the recording process. The subtitle "(She's So Heavy)" was appended during one of the final sessions, when the trio of John, Paul and George were layering the chorus harmonies.

"As in 'Don't Let Me Down', the love described has as much to do with the pain of longing as it does with the joy of fulfillment," wrote Tim Riley. "John's yearning has a long history, but his relationship with Yoko conjures up the most profound fears – anxieties about closeness that were first heard in 'If I Fell' and 'Girl', and later more imposingly in 'She Said She Said' and 'Julia'. By making the simple declaration of 'I Want You' a testimonial of faith as well as a howl of doubt, with none of the parody he tried to hide behind in 'Yer Blues', he transforms his idiomatic blues into a statement of purpose... [but] in the end, the tension is chopped off rather than resolved – Lennon seeks absolution and finds only continuous struggle."

Ian Macdonald underscores the song's connection to "Don't Let Me Down", first calling "I Want You" a "brutally uncompromising Lennon creation – about as far from the plaintive, sentimental vein of McCartney's recent ballads as it was possible to get.

"Sharing more than an urge to plumb the depths, these songs are, in effect, two halves of a single statement: 'Don't let me down' because 'I want you,'" he wrote. "Lennon's passion for Ono has shaken him to the core. His long dreamed-of erotic mother had finally arrived and the reality was almost too much for her. Sexually addicted to her, he was helplessly dependent, a predicament grindingly explicit in his chord sequence: the sickening plunge from E7 to B♭7; the augmented A that drags his head up to make him go through it all again; the hammering flat ninth that collapses, spent, on the song's insatiable Dm arpeggio.

"Nightmarishly tormented," he concluded, "this is a musical tryst with a succubus. No wonder the lyric consists of the same phrase over and over again. Lennon is literally obsessed." No kidding.

Shown to the band during the *Get Back* sessions, the song's recording began the following month in the earliest days of *Abbey Road*, on February 22, 1969. It was worked on in two April sessions, on the 18th and 20th, with the final sessions on August 8 and 11. Its mixdown on August 20 was the last time the Beatles ever assembled in the studio together.

"The Ballad of John and Yoko"

John's final love song as a Beatle could not have been more perfect. After the myriad emotional expectorations of the *White Album* and the let-me-be-perfectly-clear mania of "Don't Let Me Down" and "I Want You", he returns to his most tried-and-true format – autobiography – and gives the world some good news, for a change.

The good news was, of course, that John and Yoko had married, and that their new mission in life was to Give Peace a Chance – a theme that would define them for some time to come. The song itself, a straight-up, blues-riff pop-rocker, is practically a travelogue of their 1969 wedding trip, as they scrambled toward the altar and beyond:

Standing in the dock at Southampton
Tryin' to get to Holland or France
The man in the mac said, "You've got to go back"
You know, they didn't even get us a chance

Finally made the plane into Paris
Honeymooning down by the Seine
Peter Brown called to say
"You can make it okay
You can get married in Gibraltar near Spain"

...and so on, punctuating each stage of the journey with

Christ, you know it ain't easy
You know how hard it can be
The way things are goin'
They're gonna crucify me

The frenetic journey continues, as they do the bed-in for peace in Amsterdam, then proceed to Vienna and then, finally,

Caught the early plane back to London
Fifty acorns tied in a sack
The men from the press said, "We wish you success
It's good to have the both of you back"

As he was leaving the Beatles, John was sounding downright... healthy. He wasn't, of course, and that would become all too apparent four years later in Los Angeles; but as the curtain begins to fall on his band, he has at least found a functional equilibrium with his new love, identified a productive focus for his energies. And, in the session for the single, had one final joyous musical moment with his longtime partner and friend – John and Paul recorded the song together, without the other two.[53]

Even so, the narcissism of the whole thing did not go unnoticed by the press, which rolled its eyes at the couple's attention-grabbing peace promotions. The song became emblematic of this new behavior, per Ian Macdonald:

"Behaving as if they personally invented peace, they jetted round the world in first-class seats selling it at third-rate media-events. This was arrogant as well as silly, and the news media's derision, of which 'The Ballad of John and Yoko' self-righteously complains, was not only inevitable but, in the main, justified."

Recorded April 14, 1969, "The Ballad of John and Yoko" was the last Beatles single to go to #1 in their homeland, despite being banned there by the BBC.

---

[53] John did the lead vocal, guitars and percussion; Paul played drums and bass, piano, maracas, and did the harmony vocal. (George was out of the country at the time, and Ringo was away filming *The Magic Christian*.)

From Me to You: The Lovely Linda

Most of what Paul would write for his new wife would appear after the breakup of the Beatles. "The Lovely Linda" would rapidly surface on *McCartney*, the premiere solo album released in April 1970. "My Love" would follow three years later, once Wings was up and running, on the album *Red Rose Speedway*.

But he did work one in before the end of the Beatles, during the *Get Back* sessions – some of which Linda, as well as daughter Heather, attended.

The one he worked in was "Two of Us" - the opening track of *Let It Be*.

"'Two of Us' sounds like a song about their Liverpool teenage years together – burning matches, lifting latches, and going home to play more music together," wrote Steve Turner, "but the 'two of us' were not Paul and John but Paul and Linda.

"One of the most attractive things to Paul about his new girlfriend was her unpretentious 'hang-loose' approach to everything. In a life restricted by schedules and contractual obligations, he relished being with someone who seemed consistently laid-back, someone with whom he could forget he was a Beatle."

"As a kid I loved getting lost. I would say to my father – let's get lost," Turner quoted Linda as saying. "But you could never seem to be able to get really lost. All signs would eventually lead back to New York or wherever we were staying! Then, when I moved to England to be with Paul, we would put Martha in the back of the car and drive out of London. As soon as we were on the open road I'd say, 'Let's get lost' and we'd keep driving without looking at any signs. Hence the line in the song, 'Two of us going nowhere'. Paul wrote 'Two of Us' on one of those days out. It's about us. We just pulled off in a wood somewhere and parked the car. I went off walking while Paul sat in the car and started writing. He also mentions the postcards because we used to send a lot of postcards to each other".

Still, intimations that John lives somewhere in the lyric remain.

"...when the key jumps unexpectedly to wistful B flat for its six-bar middle, the lyric seems to be more to do with Paul and John than Paul and Linda," wrote Ian Macdonald. "The lines about chasing paper and getting nowhere are usually taken to refer to The Beatles' contractual troubles, which escalated into a full-blown lawsuit two days after the *Get Back* sessions ended."

Kenneth Womack finds more of John: *"You and I have memories / Longer than the road that stretches out ahead...* It's a bittersweet emotion that merits contemplation, if not acknowledgment, for its invariable place in the human life-cycle."

Even so, Linda's testimony trumps the learned speculations of Fab Four scholars; it can be her song, and still hold callbacks to the love that preceded her.

And she hardly goes without, as the future unfolds: in addition to "The Lovely Linda" and "My Love", "Every Night", "Man Was We Lonely", "Long Haired Lady", "A Love for You", "I Am Your Singer", "Some People Never Know" - and, of course, the magnificent "Maybe I'm Amazed" will all shortly follow...

"Something"

It's fitting that George, rather than John or Paul, has the last word in the Beatles Love Song department.

Though "The Long and Winding Road" will be the last Beatles love song to go to #1, its creation predated "Something" - George's unparalleled masterpiece – by six months. The former song's charting occurred nearly 18 months after its recording, due to the shelving of the *Let It Be* album.

The crowning jewel of *Abbey Road*, then, is the true zenith of the Fab Four's love song journey.

Why so fitting? Two reasons: his rise to excellence in the love song department was the steadiest (and least self-indulgent), covering the greatest distance; and while he and Pattie would eventually crash and burn, George more than any other songwriting Beatle managed to hold it together as a boyfriend/husband longer and with less drama than John or Paul.

Written during the *White Album* sessions and built around a line nicked from James Taylor's "Something in the Way She Moves",[54] George's greatest Beatles song made its way into the *Get Back* sessions, only to be ignored by the others. He offered it to Joe Cocker, who promptly recorded it for his album *Joe Cocker!*

It finally took shape in the *Abbey Road* sessions, where the basic tracks were recorded on May 2 and 5 of 1969. George Martin's praise was unequivocal:

"It took my breath away," he said later, "mainly because I never thought George could do it – it was a tremendous work and so simple."

Simple it was indeed, with three short verses, each ending with a refrain, and a soaring middle-eight that yielded to one of the finest guitar solos of George's career.

Ringo's marvelous tom rolls, Paul's rushing-heart bass and George's own hooks enter into an exquisite dance, wrapping

---

[54]"If George either consciously or unconsciously took a line from one of my songs, then I find it very flattering," Taylor said.

George's earnest lyric in a comforting cocoon of gentle light and motion:

Something in the way she moves
Attracts me like no other
Something in the way she woos me

I don't wanna leave her now
You know I believe and how

Ian Macdonald: "...the song contains, in its second verse, its author's finest lines – at once deeper and more elegant than almost anything his colleagues ever wrote."

Somewhere in her smile she knows
That I don't need no other lover
Something in her style that shows me

George Martin provided an exemplary string score that lifts the song, already majestic, into the clouds. His orchestration is warm and soaring – nothing like the cloying sonic melodrama that Phil Spector's strings and choir will inflict on Paul's "The Long and Winding Road" in the following year.

Kenneth Womack called the song "a stunning apex... 'Something' would be Harrison's crowning achievement and the classic tune that Frank Sinatra would famously dub 'the greatest love song of the past fifty years.'"[55]

"For all the predictable dismissals the schmaltzy tone baits, the high [musical] drama between George, Paul, and Ringo is the sound of intimacy itself," Tim Riley wrote. "George's romanticism has a stately touch, and this survives as his strongest since "If I Needed Someone".

Paul felt it was *Abbey Road*'s strongest cut[56] (released alongside John's "Come Together", it was George's first A-side):

---

[55]t is one of the great Beatle ironies that Sinatra famously misattributed the song to John and Paul.

"George's 'Something' was out of left field," he later said. "It was about Pattie, and it appealed to me because it has a very beautiful melody and is a really structured song. I thought it was great."

Was it about Pattie? Here again, a Beatle waffles:

"I just wrote it and then somebody put together a video that used some footage of me and Pattie, Paul and Linda, Ringo and Maureen and John and Yoko... actually, when I wrote it I was thinking of Ray Charles."

In her autobiography, Pattie takes issue with that:

"He told me, in a matter-of-fact way, that he had written it for me," she wrote. "I thought it was beautiful – and it turned out to be the most successful song he ever wrote."[57]

Her favorite version of the song, she went on to say, was the one he played for her privately in the kitchen at Kinfauns.

---

[56] So did John.

[57] It is the most covered song in the Beatles canon, behind "Yesterday". In addition to Joe Cocker, it was recorded by Ray Charles (whom George originally had in mind to sing it), James Brown, Lena Horne, Ike and Tina Turner, Elvis Presley, Barbara Mandrell, the O'Jays, Smokey Robinson, Johnny Rodriguez, Shirley Bassey, and most notoriously Frank Sinatra (twice).

1970:

Christ, You Know It Ain't Easy

From Me to You: John and Yoko

Once John and Yoko were firmly established as a couple, he began expressing his sexual passion for her directly in song, as John and George had done with Jane and Pattie - and he held nothing back. Each of the Beatles' final three albums contains a metaphorically-rich homage to his intimate fixation, showcasing his long-established knack for vivid imagery. And, for good measure, he tossed in an autobiographical single.

"Happiness is a Warm Gun" (*The White Album*). Well-known as a TV/newspaper junkie, John had taken some of his best bits from both, including most of his *Sgt. Pepper* input ("Good Morning, Good Morning", "A Day in the Life"). Along came an advertisement in an American gun magazine, suggesting the title phrase, (it was the slogan of the NRA) and off John went, scribbling furiously.

The metaphors flowed, *"warm gun"* being the stand-out with his phallic symbolism. *"When I hold you in my arms, and I feel my finger on your trigger"* – a clitoral reference – was surpassed only by the seamless perfection of the backing vocals on the chorus, *"Bang bang shoot shoot"* (thrust, thrust, ejaculate, ejaculate). And *"Mother Superior jump the gun"*? Woman-on-top.

The BBC banned the song as a result.

"Don't Let Me Down" (*Let It Be*). More straightforward (as were all the songs on *Let It Be*), a verse of this tune was a blunt statement of John's sexual fulfillment as Yoko's partner: *"I guess nobody ever really done me / Ooh she done me / She done me good..."*

"I Want You (She's So Heavy)" (*Abbey Road*). Rivaling any hard rock track produced by any band up to that point, "I Want You" is pure, unadulterated sex, consisting of only 15 words: *"I want you / I want you so bad / It's driving me mad / She's so heavy..."*, repeated over and over, against a slow, very steady, thundering, pulse-like riff that builds and builds, a musical manifestation of when the woman says, *"Keep doing EXACTLY what you're doing, don't stop!!!"*

"The Ballad of John and Yoko" (1969 single). This "wedding album" song doesn't contain the expressions of passion in the other three, and isn't a song where John sings to Yoko. As with many of Paul's Jane songs, it's a tune where John is telling the world about Yoko. It's more than that, however; the you-and-me-against-the-world tone of John's narrative is a first, among Beatles love songs. It's almost impossible to pronoun it; the story is about We, but John is singing as Me, and he's singing to the listener, not to any specific You. In terms of the message it sends – John is firmly establishing their married couplehood, in a way that very much presents them as a team. In the canon of Beatles love songs, that's refreshing; it may make this the best of John's four Yoko songs.

"The Long and Winding Road"

It's Paul who turns out the lights, serving up the Beatles' final #1 single (in the US) and its last love song on the radio – a gorgeous, enduring tune that tells of a journey. And he'd certainly been on one.

It was originally a very simple ballad, almost humble, the lament of a wandering soul for a lost love, clinging to hope – underscored by equally simple accompaniment. That changed during the final production of *Let It Be*, but the overproduced overdubs don't erase the longing Paul expresses for that winding road – in fact, Highway B842 in Scotland, which runs down Kintyre's east coast to Campbelltown - which leads to his farm, the refuge he would seek and share with Linda when the Beatles collapsed.

Paul had written that song at the farm, unsurprisingly, and had noodled it out during the early *Get Back* sessions at Twickenham Studios. His intent wasn't so much to write about a woman (the song is decidedly *not* an ode to Linda), but to write about the journey toward "the unattainable; the door you never quite reach; the road that you never get to the end of," as he told biographer Barry Miles.

Those are subtler intentions that the lyrics purport:

The long and winding road
That leads to your door
Will never disappear
I've seen that road before
It always leads me here
Lead me to your door

The second verse teases at autobiography:

The wild and windy night
That the rain washed away
Has left a pool of tears
Crying for the day

Why leave me waiting here?
Let me know the way

The wistfulness and melancholy are palpable; the song doesn't need historical subtext to be relatable. It's about longing, the need for resolution, and pushback in the indifferent beauty of the world; that imagery, which includes wind and rain, projects a sense of lostness. The long-and-winding road itself is presented as an enduring hope.

Paul's version of the song, recorded January 26, 1969 during the *Get Back* sessions, didn't surface until the *Let It Be – Naked* remix of 2003. The version that went to #1 emerged from the Phil Spector overdub session more than a year later – April Fool's Day, 1970.[58]

---

[58] So intense was Paul's rage over Spector's unwanted tampering with his song that he listed it as one of six reasons presented to the English High Court for the dissolution of the Beatles partnership.

Swan Songs

The Beatles' final three love-song singles - #1 hits, all – were evenly distributed among the three writers: John's "The Ballad of John and Yoko", George's "Something", and Paul's "The Long and Winding Road".

There's a poignancy and irony to this, when the substance of each of the three songs is considered.

John's breezy wedding album of a song is markedly different, as noted above, from his previous two Yoko songs - "Don't Let Me Down" and "I Want You". Those songs are anxious and tense, even desperate. "The Ballad of John and Yoko", on the other hand, is upbeat and – well, not quite relaxed, but certainly not tense. Rather than barfing up a tortured confession, it calls to mind the squirmy and relatable experience of having to sit through a good friend's vacation slide show. It gives us a whole new John, one we've never seen or even imagined before.

In "Something", we likewise see a George we've never seen before; confident, serene, purposeful – offering the world a window into a man's love for his woman that would make anyone wish for such a woman, such a love. Many Beatle love songs had evinced vulnerability within passion before, but never with such earnestness and warmth. And he did it in spite of his domineering bandmates, earning their enthusiastic support through the compelling power and brilliance of what he'd created.

And Paul's long and winding road, however abstract in the reading, is much like John's "Ballad" - a real-world journey into somewhere; he just hasn't taken it yet. He reintroduces longing into the mix, and this moment in the band's story wouldn't complete without it.

Consider the premise that these three love songs, each a meaningful culmination of their respective journeys as boyfriends and husbands, takes its writer in a new direction – a direction that leads them out of the Beatles.

For John, that direction is clearly Yoko. Now that they're married, and he's found purpose and focus once again, he doesn't need the Beatles. They will be fine without him, and his life is about to add many more verses to the "Ballad" travelogue.

For George, whose marriage to Pattie might be imperfect and ultimately doomed, the direction is George Harrison – an artist with his own brand, earned the hard way. "Something" cleared the path for *All Things Must Pass* and "My Sweet Lord" and the Concert for Bangladesh. He will, not un-ironically, be the first solo Beatle to score a #1 album and a #1 hit single.

For Paul, that direction is Scotland. He will go back to the egg for a season with his new family, which will welcome daughter Mary – named, appropriately, after his departed mother – and from that season will emerge a new band that will continue the work he'd hoped the Beatles would complete.

Three songs – three directions – three Beatles about to be Beatles no longer, but world-class artists on their own... with many more love songs in them.

And In the End...

How did these stories end?

As noted above, both John and Paul ended their Beatles tenure with the woman they were meant to be with, having (ultimately happy marriages). In John's case, that happiness was preceded by his "lost weekend," an 18-month separation from Yoko in Los Angeles (mostly) in which he went largely out of control, drinking heavily and carousing with the likes of Harry Nilsson. He managed to crank out the albums *Walls and Bridges* and *Rock 'n' Roll*, get his first #1 single (the last Beatle to do so) "Whatever Gets You Through the Night", and collaborate with Elton John, making his final public appearance as an artist at Madison Square Garden in 1974. But he then settled into the domestic bliss that Paul was experiencing with Linda – who toured the world with him in Wings.

George's marriage to Pattie would deteriorate in the face of her relationship with Eric Clapton; George retaliated by having a relationship with Ringo's wife Maureen in 1972. They finally divorced in 1977.

The following year, George married Olivia Arias, and the two had a son, Dhani. They had a long and happy family life until George's death in 2001.

Ringo struggled to find success as a solo artist after the breakup (though he eventually made it), becoming severely alcoholic and making a lame attempt at suicide. Maureen hung in there until 1975, when she finally divorced him for his many infidelities. She lived another 19 years, dying of leukemia in 1994.

Ringo went on to marry actress Barbara Bach in 1981; their marriage persists today, more than 40 years later.

When Pattie married Eric Clapton in 1979, every Beatle but John attended (he hadn't been invited, but said he'd have been there if he had).

Dot Rhone immigrated to Toronto Canada, and was visited by Paul when Wings played there; he sent a limo to pick her and her family up and bring them to Maple Leaf Gardens, where the band was playing, and welcomed them backstage.

Cynthia died of cancer in 2015.

The Beatles Guide to Love & Sex

Appendix: Beatlestats

First Beatle married: John, to Cynthia, on August 23, 1962

Last Beatle married: Paul, to Linda, on March 12, 1969

Most marriages: Paul (3: Linda, Heather Mills, Nancy Shevell)

Most children: Paul (4, counting adopted daughter Heather; Ringo tied with Paul at 3, counting actual children)

Premarital pregnancies: 4 (Cynthia with John; Dot with Paul; Maureen with Ringo; Yoko with John)

Most prolific love song muse: Jane (11, within Beatles); Pattie (9, Beatles and beyond)

First grandfather: Ringo (Tatia Jayne Starkey, 9/6/1985)

First great-grandfather: Ringo (Stone Zakamo Low, 8/14/2016)

Appendix:
The Best Beatles Album to Have Sex To

Fans of a certain age will remember the early Seventies, a singular era when psychedelia had let album-oriented rock into our bedrooms, where sexual soundtracks augmented erotic action lit by lava lamps.

The pacesetter among those soundtracks was Pink Floyd's *Dark Side of the Moon*, by far the most well-suited to the purpose, with its gradually-intensifying rhythms, ethereal moods and the ecstatic female utterances of "The Great Gig in the Sky". More babies were conceived to *DSofM* than any other 50 rock albums you might name, can we agree?

The interminable but substantial *Yessongs*, a three-disc live excursion into karmic bliss that emotes like crazy and enjoys dynamics more intense than *Tristan Und Isolde*, might be the strongest second place. Honorable mentions to Steely Dan's *Aja*, for copulating intellectuals, Fleetwood Mac's *Rumours* if you're having break-up sex, and *Tusk*, if it's just mindless animal lust.

What if you're a die-hard Beatles fan? What album (let's settle for an album side) most enhances copulation?

We can safely write off the first five albums or so, I think. Not much mood music there, and a vibrator-like sameness when it comes to structure and energy. Let's look farther downline, into the studio era.

Revolver? Side One is a potential foreplay paradise, with the shifting grooves and tempi of "Taxman", "Eleanor Rigby", "I'm Only Sleeping" and the moody "Love You To". It's practically a tease manual! Until you get to that vibe-killing "Yellow Submarine" and reach for the remote.

Side Two? All over the place, no consistent groove, until "Tomorrow Never Knows", which certainly has erotic potential – almost hypnotic. We're better off just playing that one eight times in a row, probably.

What about *Magical Mystery Tour*? There's some promising diddle to be found in the title track, to be sure, and the moody procession of "The Fool on the Hill", "Flying", and "Blue Jay Way" probably make for the kind of steadily-building energy you want in a truly great shag. And the side ends with "I Am the Walrus", which is arguably a really strong climax. But between them, we stumble into "Your Mother Should Know"... and none of us wants that.

Surely the trusty *White Album* has potential?

We can write off Sides Two and Four up front. The former has little energy in its early tracks, and "I Will" and "Julia" will put us right to sleep when we should be at our peak (and you have to listen to Ringo in the middle).[59] The latter, well, "Revolution No. 9", complete with Yoko intoning, "You become naked." Could there be a bigger buzz-kill?

Side Three has some promise, opening with the raucous "Birthday" and the rompy "Yer Blues" - good foreplay tunes! - and ends with "Helter Skelter", certainly a great finish; but in between you've got "Mother Nature's Son" and "Sexy Sady", which are like stopping for phone calls from your aunt. And "Everybody's Got Something to Hide Except Me and My Monkey", well... that's like somebody farting during oral sex.

If there's a *White Album* side to have sex to, it would be Side One, don't you think? "Back in the USSR" has that bodice-ripping energy, and there's a long French kiss moment in "Dear Prudence", and the thread of "Glass Onion" and "Ob-La-Di, Ob-La-Da" make for a steady build-up rhythm. And, hey, what could be better that "While My Guitar Gently Weeps" for the home stretch, with its literal moaning and wailing, followed by "Happiness is a Warm Gun" (which is an *actual metaphor* for orgasm!)?

Yeah, we almost get there, except for that idiotic "Wild Honey Pie", which destroys whatever rhythm we're getting from its predecessors, followed by "Bungalow Bill", which stumbles rhythmically like a drunk on an ice patch. And Yoko.

---

[59]We're obliged to acknowledge "Why Don't We Do It in the Road" on this side, which is of course tone-perfect for the moment; but with its duration of 1:41, it might create confidence issues.

Abbey Road is promising at first. I mean, there's no song title in the entire Beatles canon more shag-minded than "Come Together", right? "Something" is certainly a mood-builder, and "I Want You (She's So Heavy)" might have been a direct inspiration of *Dark Side of the Moon* itself, as deeply passionate and hypnotic as anything the Beatles ever recorded. But then, "Maxwell's Silver Hammer". And "Octopus's Garden". Nope. Nope.

Side Two? Well, what woman wouldn't want to be felt up to "Here Comes the Sun"? And "Because" is certainly a long-kiss tune. The medley is a masterpiece of mounting energy and steadily-building rhythms, itself ending very climactically.

But then... Queen Elizabeth. Nope. Nope.

But we have a refuge, Gentle Reader.

Sgt. Pepper's Lonely Hearts Club Band.

Side One looks good on paper; the two opening tracks – the title tune and "With a Little Help from My Friends" - have lots of support for good feel-up; and "Lucy in the Sky with Diamonds" is a great long-kiss tune. "Fixing a Hole" takes on a whole new meaning, and the bouncy "Getting Better" sets a good tempo for what comes next. Ah, but then "She's Leaving Home" takes us all ¾, and that just doesn't work, and "Being for the Benefit of Mr. Kite" ruins everything, because clowns.

But there's Side Two!

"Within You Without You". Most people don't much like this track, but what a *great* make-out tune! It's all loopy, hypnotic energy. A great start, and then "When I'm Sixty-Four" - well, playful just works, when you're on your way but not quite getting down to it. "Lovely Rita" actually has heavy breathing and an orgasm *built in* – certainly inspiring! - and "Good Morning Good Morning" has just the right tempo and punch (if you can brush aside the barnyard imagery). Then comes the "Pepper" reprise, with its rapid pulse and soaring crescendo – followed by "A Day in the Life", with its built-in tease pauses and two – count 'em, *two!* - musical orgasms, in the frenetic orchestra swells. Then there's that hyperextended E chord on the piano at the end – the perfect afterbliss!

What more could anyone ask for?

Your Kindly Author, then, enthusiastically recommends *Pepper* Side Two as your next sexual soundtrack. Try it out and report back!

Appendix: Beatle Babies

Julian Lennon (b. April 8, 1963) is the oldest of the Beatle children, son of John and first wife Cynthia Lennon. Describing his famous dad as "more of a wise uncle" than a father, he followed in his footsteps, becoming a pop musician in his own right.

Perhaps the most inspirational of the Beatles children (apart from his younger brother Sean), he prompted the writing of John's 'Lucy in the Sky with Diamonds' with a crayon drawing, and got Paul started on 'Hey Jude' when Paul once dropped in on him for a visit.

Zak Starkey (b. September 13, 1965) is Ringo's oldest, one of three children he had with first wife Maureen Cox. Like the Lennon boys, Zak followed in his father's footsteps, receiving drum lessons from Keith Moon and has played with Spencer Davis Group, Iron Maiden, The Who, Oasis, and his father.

"I love my dad, but being Ringo's son is the biggest drag in my life," he once said. "It's a total pain."

Zak made Ringo the first grandBeatle when his daughter was born in 1985.

Jason Starkey (b. August 19, 1967), born in the Summer of Love, likewise plays drums, although his career is more low-key. He has played with various regional bands in and around London and Brighton.

Mary McCartney (b. August 28, 1969), the first child of Paul and Linda, followed in her mother's footsteps, rather than her father's. Mary has had a long and successful career as a photographer, has done a number of notable celebrity portraits and worked in television. She currently works for her father at MPL Communications.

She can be seen on the back cover of Paul's first solo album *McCartney* as an infant, nestled inside his jacket.

Lee Starkey (b. November 11, 1970) had a tougher time than her brothers settling on a career. She worked at Tower Records and the Hard Rock Café before learning to be a make-up artist, and in recent years has moved into fashion design. She successfully fought a battle with cancer in the mid-Nineties.

Stella McCartney (b. September 13, 1971), Paul and Linda's second child, grew up on the road with Wings but displayed sensibilities more tuned to working-class Liverpool. Scrappy and aggressive, she entered the world of fashion design and has enjoyed considerable success.

Sean Lennon (b. October 9, 1975), the son of John and Yoko, grew up collaborating with his mother, appearing on her solo albums, and co-wrote with Lenny Kravitz at age 16. He has recorded and toured extensively, in his own band and as a guest with others, and is the most versatile of the Beatle progeny, playing guitar, bass, piano and drums. He was in the cast of Michael Jackson's *Moonwalker* in 1998 ... and his godfather is Elton John.

James McCartney (b. September 12, 1977), last child of Paul and Linda, picked up both guitar and pen from his father, playing as well as composing. He played on his father's albums *Flaming Pie* and *Driving Rain*, and has released two solo EPs.

Dhani Harrison (b. August 1, 1978), the only child of George (with second wife Olivia), carried on the Beatle offspring tradition by taking up the guitar (Ringo frightened him away from the drums, scaring him badly in early childhood by playing very loudly). Appropriately, Dhani is named after the sixth and seventh notes of the Indian music scale ('dha' and 'ni').

Dhani had a very close relationship with his father, and helped complete George's final album *Brainwashed* with Jeff Lynne after his father's death. He performed in Eric Clapton's *Concert for George* tribute, has since formed his own band, and was a key figure in the creation of *The Beatles: Rock Band* video game.

Beatrice McCartney (b. October 28, 2003), the daughter of Paul and second wife Heather Mills, is perhaps the last of the Beatle children.

Heather McCartney (b. December 31, 1962), is the adopted daughter of Paul McCartney.

Appendix: *Love Songs*

Label	Capitol (US), Parlophone (UK)
Released	10/21/1977 (UK)
	11/19/1977 (UK)
Chart Position	#7 UK Albums Chart
	#24 US Billboard 200
Sales	3,000,000+ (US)

It was the Year of *Star Wars*, the Year of Jimmy Carter, the Year of the Apple II. The Clash debuted; the Sex Pistols were dropped by EMI; and Fleetwood Mac released *Rumours*, the album of the decade.

And in Beatleland, Paul was releasing "Mull of Kintyre," one of his most beloved singles; John was raising a toddler in New York City; George was breaking up with his wife Pattie; and Ringo was trying his hand at disco.

Against this quirky historical backdrop emerged a wondrous Beatles compilation, a double album spanning the band's entire history and showcasing the songs it had always done best: songs of love.

Gathering up 24 of the Beatles' best love songs and throwing in a Buddy Holly song ("Words of Love," which the band had covered on *Beatles for Sale* 13 years earlier), Capitol created a lavish offering with a simulated leather cover and a stylish 11x11" lyric booklet done in calligraphy on simulated parchment. The image of the Beatles, done in simulated gold foil, was based on their 1967 *Look Magazine* portrait by Richard Avedon.

Tracks

Side One
Yesterday
I'll Follow the Sun
I Need You

Girl
In My Life
Words of Love
Here, There and Everywhere

Side Two
Something
And I Love Her
If I Fell
I'll Be Back
Tell Me What You See
Yes It Is

Side Three
Michelle
It's Only Love
You're Going to Lose That Girl
Every Little Thing
For No One
She's Leaving Home

Side Four
The Long and Winding Road
This Boy
Norwegian Wood (This Bird Has Flown)
You've Got to Hide Your Love Away
I Will
P.S. I Love You

    The collection is superb, a well-deserved commercial success, serving as a thoughtful compendium of the staggering talent of the Fab Four. It features their very best – Paul's "Yesterday," the most covered song of all time, and "Something," famously called "the greatest love song ever written" by Frank Sinatra. It travels from "P.S. I Love You," the second song they ever recorded as a group, to "The Long and Winding Road," the final #1 single released before the band ended.

The songs touch on every aspect of love and romance explored during their years as a band, from romantic longing ("And I Love Her") to deep reflection ("In My Life") to anxiety ("Girl") to infidelity ("Norwegian Wood"). It includes George's earnest proclamation "I Need You" and John's Dylanesque, multi-layered "You've Got to Hide Your Love Away" (said to be an observation on the closeted life of the gay Brian Epstein – see "John and Brian" and "You've Got to Hide Your Love Away" above).

The songs include fictional women ("Michelle") and real ones (Pattie Boyd in "I Need You," Jane Asher in "Every Little Thing"), and showcases several songs previously obscure to most fans ("I'll Be Back," "Tell Me What You See").

Not every song seems to fit in – "She's Leaving Home" doesn't seem to be a love song in the conventional sense at all – but for sheer stylistic and narrative depth and breadth, no other Beatles compilation compares.

Love Out of Sync

Wisely, Capitol did not sequence the album either chronologically or thematically. The two discs are a Beatle stew, thoroughly mixed but certainly not random. The result is a stylistic potpourri that stirs the ear, often invoking Beatles eras in surprising patterns. Side Four, for instance, calendars out like this:

The Long and Winding Road (1970)
This Boy (1963)
Norwegian Wood (1965)
You've Got to Hide Your Love Away (1965)
I Will (1968)
P.S. I Love You (1962)

That's a jump from *Let It Be* to *Meet the Beatles*, from *Rubber Soul* to *Help!*, from *The White Album* to *Please Please Me* – a musical scrapbook of sound and emotions and history.

Abandoned Single

Initially, there had been a plan by Capitol to issue a single to promote the compilation. It would have been "Girl," which originally appeared on *Rubber Soul*, with "You're Going to Lose That Girl" as the B-side. That plan got as far as the printing of sleeves for the record, but in October it was cancelled.

Ratings

The *Rolling Stone* Record Guide gives *Love Songs* 4 stars out of 5. *AllMusic* is less generous at 2.5.

The album went 3x platinum in the US. But, curiously, it sold only 60,000 copies in the Beatles' homeland (while selling 100,000 in Canada).

It remained on the US charts for 31 weeks.

Bibliography / Recommended Reading

Book Sources

All the Songs: The Story Behind Every Beatles Release, Guesdon, Jean-Michel et al. Black Dog &Leventhal, 2013

All Things Must Pass Away: Harrison, Clapton, and Other Assorted Love Songs, Womack, Kenneth &Kruppa, Jason. Chicago Review Press, 2021

*BEATLE! The Pete Best Story*Best, Pete; Doncaster, Patrick. Plexus Publishing, 1985

Beatle Wives: The Women the Men We Loved Fell in Love With, Shapiro, Marc. Riverdale Avenue Books, 2021

Beatleness, Leonard, Candy. Arcade, 2016

The Beatles A-Z, Friede, Goldie, et al. Methuen, 1980

The Beatles Anthology, The Beatles, Chronicle Books, 2000

The Beatles as Musicians: Revolver *through the* Anthology, Everett, Walter. Oxford University Press, 1999

The Beatles: The Biography, Spitz, Bob. Back Bay Books, 2006

The Beatles Day by Day: A Chronology, Lewisohn, Mark. Harmony Books, 1987

The Beatles Recording Sessions: The Official Story of the Abbey Road Years, Lewisohn, Mark. Harmony Books, 1988

Beatlesongs, Dowlding, William J. Fireside, 1989

Behind Sad Eyes: The Life of George Harrison, Shapiro, Marc. St. Martin's Griffin, 2001

Body Count, Schwartz, Francie. Straight Arrow Books, 1972

The Classical Beatles: Finding Mozart, Beethoven and Bach in the Fab Four Canon, Robinson, Scott. Paleos Media, 2022

A Hard Day's Write, Turner, Steve. Harper, 2005

John, Lennon, Cynthia. Three Rivers Press, 2006

John Lennon: The Life, Norman, Philip. Little, Brown and Company, 2009.

Lennon, Coleman, Ray. McGraw-Hill, 1985

Lennon: The Man, The Myth, The Music – The Definitive Life, Riley, Tim. Hyperion, 2011

The Lives of John Lennon, Goldman, Albert. William Morrow & Company, 1988

Lucy in the Mind of Lennon: An Empirical Analysis of Lucy in the Sky with Diamonds, Tim Kasser. Oxford University Press, 2014

McCartney: The Definitive Biography, Salewicz, Chris. St Martin's Press, 1986

Magical Mystery Tours: My Life with the Beatles, Bramwell, Tony & Kingsland, Rosemary. Thomas Dunne Books, 2005

Men, Masculinity and The Beatles, King, Martin. Routledge, 2013

The Quotable Beatles: A Compendium of the Fab Four's Wisdom, Insight, Humor and Irreverence, Robinson, Scott. Paleos Media, 2011

Paul McCartney: The Life, Norman, Philip. Little, Brown and Company, 2016.

The Progressive Beatles: The Art Rock Hidden in the Canon of the World's Greatest Band, Robinson, Scott. Paleos Media, 2020

Revolution in the Head: The Beatles Records and the Sixties, Macdonald, Ian. Chicago Review Press, 2007

Ringo: With a Little Help, Starr, Michael et al. Backbeat, 2016

Rock Candy: The Beatles, Robinson, Scott. Paleos Media, 2012

Tell Me Why: The Beatles Album by Album, Song by Song, The Sixties and After. Riley, Tim. Knopf, 1988

Tune In: The Beatles – All These Years, Lewisohn, Mark. Crown, 2016.

A Twist of Lennon, Lennon, Cynthia. Avon Books, 1980

The Ultimate Beatles Encyclopedia, Harry, Bill. MJF Books, 1992

Wonderful Tonight: George Harrison, Eric Clapton and Me, Boyd, Pattie. Crown, 2008

The Words and Music of George Harrison. Inglis, Ian. Praeger, 2010

Yesterday: The Unauthorized Biography of Paul McCartney, Flippo, Chet. Doubleday, 1988

Internet Sources

"Don't Pass Me By". *The Beatles Bible*. 15 March 2008.

Magazine Sources

John Lennon interview, *Playboy*, Sept. 1980

John Lennon interview, *Rolling Stone*, Dec. 1970

John Lennon interview, *Rolling Stone*, Dec. 1980

"Taped 'Diary' of John Lennon Unearthed", *Rolling Stone*, April 1999

"Love Them Do: The Story of the Beatles' Biggest Fans – Revisiting the Little-Known History of the Apple Scruffs", *Rolling Stone*, Feb 2014

About the Author

Scott Robinson is a journalist, social scientist, public speaker and musician, and was for 20 years a music critic with the Louisville Courier-Journal. He has also been published in *Rolling Stone* and *The Wall Street Journal*. He can be found at

scott.robinson@glenmillscience.com

www.ingramcontent.com/pod-product-compliance
Lightning Source LLC
Chambersburg PA
CBHW031614210526
45464CB00004B/1571